MAX WEBER CLASSIC MONOGRAPHS

Selected and with new introductions by Bryan S. Turner

T0347962

MAX WEBER CLASSIC
MONOGRAPHS

MAX WEBER CLASSIC MONOGRAPHS

Volume V: Max Weber and Modern Sociology

A. Sahay

With an introduction by Bryan S. Turner

London and New York

First published in 1971
by Routledge & Kegan Paul Ltd

Reprinted in 1998
by Routledge
2 Park Square, Milton Park, Abingdon, Oxfordshire OX14 4RN

Simultaneously published in the USA and Canada
by Routledge
711 Third Avenue, New York, NY 10017

First issued in paperback 2014
Routledge is an imprint of the Taylor and Francis Group, an informa company

Transferred to Digital Printing 2006

7-volume set
Volume V ISBN 13: 978-0-415-17456-5 (hbk)
Volume V ISBN 13: 978-0-415-75731-7 (pbk)

Introduction typeset in Times by Routledge

British Library Cataloguing in Publication Data
A catalogue record for this book is available from the British Library

Library of Congress Cataloging in Publication Data
A catalogue record for this book has been requested

Publisher's note: These reprints are taken from original copies of each
book. In many cases the condition of these originals is not perfect.
The paper, often acidic and having suffered over time, and the copy
from such things as inconsistent printing pressure resulting in faint
text, show-through from one side of a leaf to the other, the filling in of
some characters, and the break-up of type. The publisher has gone to
great lengths to ensure the quality of these reprints, but wishes to
point out that certain characteristics of the original copies will, of
necessity, be apparent in reprints thereof.

INTRODUCTION

Bryan S. Turner

This study of the place of values in the sociology of Max Weber is Volume V of the Routledge and Thoemmes Press *Max Weber Classic Monographs* series. It was first published in 1971 and contains essays by distinguished Weberian scholars, whose contributions to the analysis of the nature of sociological interpretation and explanation in Weber's social theory remain an essential dimension of the contemporary debate over the philosophy of social science and methodology. John Rex's *Key Problems in Sociological Theory* (1961), which found its inspiration in Weber's sociological perspective, was a landmark in the development of the theory of social action and the emergence of so-called 'conflict sociology'. Alan Dawe's article (1970) on 'the two sociologies', which also found inspiration in Weber's approach, was a seminal text in the development of post-war social theory. In this collection by Sahay, they continue to explore key issues in sociology through an exposition of Weber's account of values. More generally, Weber's ideal type constructs have been an important framework for the more general understanding of modern society and modernity. Weber's view of capitalism as an economic system, which imposed rationalisation and discipline on everyday life, remains controversial, especially in the light of contemporary concerns about the environment and the ecology. This reprint of Arun Sahay's study is therefore an important intellectual event.

The study is important because it recognises that no account of Weber's sociology can be complete or adequate which artificially separates the issue of values and methodology from the comparative and historical studies of religion, politics and economics. Weber's analysis of the problem of the explication of values is not an optional addition or merely contingent feature of his sociology – it in fact constitutes a core issue. John Rex, exploring four different lines of thought on values and objectivity in Weber's sociology, shows that 'standpoints' can never be simply avoided (Rex, 1961), and Alan Dawe explains that values are not an obstacle to scientific research, but an essential feature of the sociological approach which attempts to concern itself with 'the interpretive understanding of social action and thereby with a causal explanation of its course and consequences' (Weber, 1978: 4). J. E. T. Eldridge's commentary, 'Weber's Approach to the Sociological Study of Industrial Workers', also demonstrates the importance of value analysis in empirical research and underlines the fact that, for Weber, no amount of quantitative data could in themselves make social phenomena 'understandable'. Robert Moore identifies the importance of economic ethics in Weber's comparative sociology of religion, thereby placing the specific studies of Protestantism in their general context.

The problem of values in Weber's sociology is, as we will see shortly, a major component of 'the tragic view of life' which haunted not only Weber's sociology, but much of the world view of late nineteenth-century German philosophy (Liebersohn, 1988). This sense of the tragic was a result of the decline of a tradition in which the calling of the cultured bourgeoisie was to achieve personal autonomy and fulfilment through education, that is through personal cultivation. In Germany, there was a clear demarcation between 'culture' which embraced personal values of discipline, training and rational enhancement of personality, and 'civilisation' which represented industrial growth, urbanisation and the dominance of technical and specialised knowledge. Civilisation was the new world of technology, standardisation and regulation. In fact, it was closely connected with Weber's understanding of rationalisation. The differentiation between culture and civilisation as value systems was widely discussed in German sociology in this period. For example, the second volume of Norbert Elias's classic inquiry *The Civilizing Process* (1982) was overtly a study of the origins of cultural norms to regulate the self. First appearing in print in 1939, it can also be read as a reflection on the decline of culture. The tragic nature of Germany within this sociological perspective was that civilisation was seen to be destructive of culture.

The German tradition of the isolated and powerless educated stratum had its origins in the eighteenth century, but it gained momentum in the nineteenth century. With the failure of the 1844 revolutions to establish a bourgeois liberal democracy, the bourgeoisie was excluded from political power. Instead they became powerful in Germany in the civil service and as carriers of educational values. While the Junker class of landowners continued to exercise power through the limited representational organs of government, the bourgeoisie established a tradition of the cultivated self and developed educational institutions which aimed at the autonomy of the personality, the cultivation of inner sensibility and feelings, and the holistic education of the complete personality. This bourgeois class was the *Bildungsburgertum*, whose primary values were organised around *Bildung* (the formation of personality through education). Their values had an origin in the legacy of the *Bildungsroman*. This genre was launched by Goethe in *Wilhelm Meister*, a novel which apart from anything else celebrates youth and youthfulness as the thematic strand of a new cultural hero. *Bildungsroman* explored the notion that the self was created by a moment of truth, which as an event is primarily interior; the romance was an inner quest for the truth of the self (Moretti, 1987). The illusions of the heroic life in this genre were explored by Georg Lukács in 1911 in *The Soul and the Forms* – a study much appreciated by Weber (Lukács, 1974).

This tradition of education and the cultivation of the self was thought to be under attack during the nineteenth century. *Bildung* or 'self-formation' was threatened by what Weber called the 'disenchantment' or secularisation of western culture by the process of rationalisation. The erosion of this special culture was related to the development of industrial capitalism, the transformation of rural communities by urbanism, the rise of the 'masses', the growing dominance of technical knowledge and scientific values, the spread of technology and the attack on the university system as elite institutions (Goldman,1992: 25). The universities were expanding, the natural sciences were growing (often at the expense of the humanities) and it was assumed that the tradition of *Bildung* could not cope with these changes. For Weber, rationalisation meant the specialisation of knowledge and the bureaucratisation of the university, which would exist merely to produce mindless specialists, or little cogs in the bureaucratic machine. The ideals which had been established by the Humboldt reforms of the university were no longer a dominant view of educational requirements in Imperial Germany. Within a social context where *Bildung* was esteemed, the university professors were crucial to this 'mandarin aristocracy', but their influence declined in the late nineteenth century, along with the erosion of the status of university education and culture (Ringer,

1969). There was a general sense of fragmentation, specialisation and cultural decline. For philosophers like Wilhelm Dilthey, the new Germany was characterised by endless, conflicting world-views (*Weltanschauungen*) which were without foundation and coherence; the old values of religion and philosophy were on the defensive.

Against this background of cultural crisis, we can more clearly see that one of the linking themes of Weber's sociology was the shaping of the self in western culture. The principal component of this sociology of the self is *The Protestant Ethic and the Spirit of Capitalism* (Weber, 1930) which first appeared in 1904 and provides a historical analysis of the impact of asceticism on the development of the modern self. The theme of personality and life-order is also present in the comparative studies of religion in which different constellations of religious culture produce different personality formations. The issues of vocations and the self also form an important aspect of the public lectures on 'science as a vocation' and 'politics as a vocation' towards the end of his life (Lassman and Velody, 1989).

Clearly Weber thought that the *Bildungsideal* was under attack from the rationalisation of culture, the disenchantment of values and the specialisation of knowledge. This differentiation of the cultural spheres would result in the bureaucratic world of competent yes-men. At the conclusion of *The Protestant Ethic and the Spirit of Capitalism* Weber noted that we were already moving into a social world of 'Specialists without spirit, sensualists without heart; this nullity imagines that it has attained a level of civilization never before achieved' (1930: 182). This specialised world is ironically the unanticipated product of the Protestant Reformation and the evolution of asceticism in everyday life. The tragic irony of these developments is a theme which constantly appears in Weber's sociology as an issue about the fatefulness of the social world, that is, about the unintended consequences of social action (Turner, 1996). Weber also agreed with Dilthey that these developments were compounded by the diversity and fragmentation of social values, which means that we live in a 'polytheistic' environment of competing and irreconcilable value systems.

Weber's analysis of this cultural crisis occurs at many points in his work, but one of the key passages is situated in the 'Intermediate reflections' (*Zwischenbetrachtung*). This passage was written in 1913 and published in 1915 in the *Archiv für Sozialwissenschaft und Sozialpolitik* as an additional introduction to the collected essays on the sociology of religion (*Gesammelte Aufsätze zur Religionssoz-*

iologie). In the final version of 1920, the section on the erotic was an addition. It was published in translation by H. Gerth and C. Wright Mills (1991: 323–59) and has become a key passage in modern interpretations of Weber by writers like Friedrich Tenbruck (1975) and Charles Turner (1992). In these 'Intermediate reflections', Weber divides culture into six value spheres: religion, economics, politics, aesthetics, the erotic and the intellectual. He examines the various tensions between an ethic brotherly love in ascetic Christianity and the various value spheres, and their various patterns of resolution. These tensions explore the contradictions between the notion of 'the world' as a normatively ideal state of affairs and the compromises which are necessary for any social order to function. By contrasting the sociology of values in these terms, Weber, following Dilthey, gave an obvious special and crucial role to religion in the shaping of western cultures. Secularisation and rationalisation have undermined the logic of these value spheres, and specialisation has meant that there can be no consistent resolution of values in the modern world.

Now this Weberian view of the rationalisation of the value spheres is often seen to be tragic and pessimistic, in the sense that Weber offers no practical solution to the dilemmas of a relativistic moral world. Karl Löwith's account (1993) of Weber is a good example. For Löwith, Weber's sociology of capitalism, like Marx's political economy, has an anthropological foundation, which is the existential condition of human beings under variable social environments. In Marx's anthropology, 'man' is alienated from the social world by private property and the division of labour, namely by a capitalist economy. For Weber, 'man' becomes a soulless and specialised creature as a result of rationalisation. However, Löwith argues that Weber merely accepts this rationalisation of society in a passive manner, while Marx's criticism of alienated society results in political action to change the world. While philosophers have merely interpreted the world, the real issue is to change the conditions of alienation by the organisation of political struggle.

There is however an alternative interpretation of Weber, which maintains that he attempts to overcome the crisis of the erosion of the tradition of *Bildungs* culture by developing a new and robust understanding of professional values through the development of two types of vocation. Weber gave two lectures in September 1918 to an audience of students at the University of Munich on the notion of a calling (*Beruf*) in science and politics. They were published in 1919 (Gerth and Mills, 1991). The lecture on politics as a vocation attempts to outline the ethic of responsibility in the world through a political vocation. It suggests that a meaningful world could be reconstituted through the creation of a viable public realm. This vocation is to combine stoicism about what is possible in political terms with a commitment to values. Weber 's intention was to call Germany's youth to the seriousness of German reconstruction without romanticism, a withdrawal into the arms of the Church or utopian radicalism.

The lecture of September 1919 on science as a vocation can be interpreted as an attempt to obtain value clarification as to the relationship between meaning and science. As with the lecture on politics, Weber sets out the limits of meaningfulness in a secular world where the religious value sphere cannot give coherence to the polytheism of values. The solution however is not mysticism but a serious quest for integrity in a life devoted to science. In both lectures, Weber avoids any suggestion that there can be an absolute solution to value relativism and any vocation will always be open to challenge and scrutiny. The point of his lecture is that science has cultural significance; it is not simply a quest for the 'facts'. The cultural conflict between the spheres can never be resolved, but the individual can gain a sense of personal integrity by engaging actively with the problems that rationalisation has created.

Sociology is of course for Weber a science and therefore sociology can be a vocation, which confronts the individual with the choices which are possible in the modern world and with the conditions under which an ethic of responsibility could be exercised. Sociology makes demands on the serious student – one of these demands is to clarify the values which they bring to the analysis of the social. Therefore the value analysis is central to empirical sociology and it is also part of the ethical conditions under which sociology seeks to be relevant to contemporary society. John Rex and Alan Dawe in their chapters in this collection by Arun Sahay implicitly lay out, through a clarification of the epistemological and philosophical demands of the social theory of Max Weber, the conditions for sociology as a vocation.

References

Antoni, C. (1959) *From History to Sociology: The transition in German historical thinking*. Detroit: Wayne State University Press.

Dawe, A. (1970) 'The two sociologies', *British Journal of Sociology*, 21: 207–18.

Elias, N. (1982) *The Civilizing Process: State formation and civilization.* Oxford: Basil Blackwell, vol. 2.

Gerth, H. H. and Mills, C. Wright (1991) *From Max Weber: Essays in sociology.* London and New York: Routledge.

Goldman, H. (1992) *Politics, Death and the Devil: Self and power in Max Weber and Thomas Mann.* Berkeley: University of California Press.

Lassman, P. and Velody, I. (eds) (1989) *Max Weber's 'Science as a Vocation'.* London: Unwin Hyman.

Liebersohn, H. (1988) *Fate and Utopia in German Sociology, 1870–1923.* Cambridge, MA: The MIT Press.

Löwith, K. (1993) *Max Weber and Karl Marx.* London: Routledge.

Lukács, G. (1974) *The Soul and its Forms.* London: Merlin.

Moretti, F. (1987) *The Way of the World: The* Bildungsroman *in European Culture.* London: Verso.

Rex, J. (1961) *Key Problems of Sociological Theory.* London: Routledge & Kegan Paul.

Ringer, F. K. (1969) *The Decline of the Mandarins: The German academic community 1890–1933.* Cambridge, MA: Harvard University Press.

Tenbruck, F. (1975) 'Das Werk Max Webers', *Koelner Zeitschrift für Soziologie,* 27: 663–702.

Turner, C. (1992) *Modernity and Politics in the Work of Max Weber.* London and New York: Routledge.

—— (1996) *For Weber: Essays on the sociology of fate.* London: Sage (2nd edition).

Weber, M. (1930) *The Protestant Ethic and the Spirit of Capitalism.* London: Unwin University Books.

—— (1978) *Economy and Society: An outline of interpretive sociology.* Berkeley: University of California Press, two volumes.

Max Weber and modern sociology

Edited by
Arun Sahay

Contributors
John Rex
Alan Dawe
Arun Sahay
Robert Moore
J. E. T. Eldrldge

Routledge & Kegan Paul
London

First published in 1971
by Routledge & Kegan Paul Ltd
2 Park Square, Milton Park, Abingdon, Oxon, OX14 4RN
270 Madison Ave, New York NY 10016
set in 10 on 12pt Pilgrim
© Routledge & Kegan Paul 1971
ISBN 7100 7169 8

Contents

Preface

This book is composed of the papers delivered at a special session of the Sociology Section (N) of the Annual Meeting of the British Association for the Advancement of Science, held at Durham on 8 September 1970, with minor revisions. The session was convened by Professor John Rex, who also contributed one of the papers, to mark the fiftieth anniversary of the death of Max Weber (1864–1920).

Professor Rex's choice of speakers formed the initial impetus for the book. It is a critical tribute to the great sociologist, with a deliberately ambiguous meaning, as fifty years after the death of a great writer one is in a better position to appraise the greatness both of the original writing and of its derivations than ever before. Weber has been the source of many derivations and a critical tribute, therefore, must mean a critique of the derivations as well as the original.

When this collection of papers was offered for publication to me as editor of *Sociological Analysis*, it seemed to demand a wider audience than the journal. The papers are published here in the order they were presented at the meeting. The editorial introduction was specially written for this book.

University of Sheffield   *A. Sahay*
  January 1971

One

Arun Sahay   **Introduction**

Max Weber needs no preliminaries of acknowledgment as the best known and most important sociological theorist today. He was primarily a theorist, because no sociologist of any attainment can remain significant without contributing to the body of theoretical ideas which properly designates a subject. In Weber's work it is impossible to separate theory from substantive analysis, although it has time and again been suggested that they must be, because Weber could not achieve the synthesis if others more recent in time cannot. Indeed, that theory and research are inseparable is one of the most important insights one gains from a systematic study and application of Weber's work, for no substantive conclusions can be valid without their quality of generalizability. In other words, whatever is concluded from an analysis, if true in the specific context, must also be true in the extension of thought to its possible connections with other contexts, facts and ideas, involved in generalization. Without this connection of inference nothing in fact is knowledge. This is what defines Weber's work, and through it, what is best in sociology. The definition of the subject is the most difficult and the most fundamental task of any intellectual pursuit. But some variation or other of the recurring theme of the nature of sociology has become, for many a facile writer, the most frequent object of fantasy as well as of supplementary livelihood.

Perhaps an attempt to discover what Weber's achievements were would not be irrelevant here, because, although Weber's many ideas have entered the currency of popular notions about society and individual and academic treatises and anthologies have frequent references to Weber, many sociologists have not become fully aware of the significance of his work, and are unable to decide what it means. A knowledge of the chronological progress of Weber's analysis[1] is an important preliminary to an understanding of his contribution to the knowledge and awareness of the modern world, it is not possible to realize either the importance or the richness of his work through such a narrative; or by simply praising and extending what one fancies in his work, as has been done in these last fifty years. The only way is to analyse its various facets in depth and to synthesize the analyses together towards a definition. This method of understanding—which Weber himself developed to an exact refinement in sociology—is particularly suited to the intricate material of the relations of facts, beliefs and ideas. The main reason for the indispensability of such a process of understanding is that nothing is tangible in 'social facts' and yet they are objective. The objectivity of social facts, which Durkheim, with such emphasis, demonstrates in his *Rules of Sociological Method*, has been misunderstood, even in Durkheim's formulation. What Durkheim emphasized was the *recognition* of social facts, but he has been interpreted as defining social reality in terms of perceptible reality. Weber, on the other hand, did not emphasize the facts of social reality, but its defining quality: value, significance and meaning; but he, too, has been misunderstood. He is interpreted as defining the subjective experience at the expense of objective observable experience.[2] These misunderstandings are to some extent difficult to overcome, because they involve unlearning some notions one has been brought up on; but they reveal, most of all, a general lack of analytical thought and awareness of its bearing upon understanding and knowledge. In Durkheim the problem of social facts remains unsolved because his sociology is almost entirely on the level of generalized description. Description invariably *presupposes* recognition of an object. Analysis, on the other hand, is completely dependent upon its correct recognition. Although Durkheim advocated successfully that social facts be recognized as independent entities, his case could only be proved by a picture of the institutions and the social structure in the theoretical framework of social facts. How social processes and movements, for example, become institutionalized—without a knowledge of which it is impossible to recognize any actual institution—was thus made irrelevant. It inevitably led to a reification of sociological concepts which persists even when we have a detailed acquaintance with Weber's work.

This important difference between Durkheim, the master of the traditional descriptive sociology—whose works are the original sources of all the current influential theories, critiques as well as empirical studies (sociographical, social psychological and social anthropological)—and Weber has not even been discerned by the writers on sociological subjects. Indeed, the criticisms of Weber which have been made in sociological literature are expressions of a bewilderment with a complete lack of deterministic principles, reified concepts and an uncompromising elimination of irrelevant factors in reaching a generalization or a definition, in his work.

Another persistent point of contrast which needs to be noted is that, although Durkheim insisted on sociological explanations being independent of psychological factors, all his own explanations are either directly psychological, as in *Suicide*, or part of a deterministic principle which can only be understood as a psychological force, however objective its social factual constituents may be. In the study of suicide, Durkheim failed to see the necessity of analysing the relationship between religious beliefs and the individual prone to a particular kind of suicide for a sociological explanation: the relationship remained fixed, the correlation established and the explanation already implicit in the principle that 'these types of conduct or thought, are not only external to the individual but are, moreover, endowed with coercive power, by virtue of which they impose themselves upon him, independent of his individual will.'[3] Therefore, the results of empirical studies will reveal—and have, in fact, revealed—nothing but more and more minute details of the psychological factors involved in suicide. Suicide as a sociological problem remains the same as it was in Durkheim's time, for the explanations which are sought of the sociological factors are inevitably straitlaced in the rigid and composite relationship of the functional or coercive nature of the beliefs which the individual is said to hold.

Weber rejected psychologism with less emphasis than Durkheim, but showed again how it cannot possibly be a rigid relationship between a stylized notion of a belief system or ideology and individual action (like suicide) but a varying and subtle one, and the sociological explanation of such a relationship needs an analysis of the relationship itself—rather than a variety of conjectures from empirical correlations on the basis of a hypothesis on what the relationship *seems* like. Weber's whole work on what is called the sociology of religion, is precisely about the relationship between world view, ethical orientation and individual action.

From such an analysis one can understand what kinds of belief can lead to a particular variety of suicide; indeed, of reform, change, revolution and even counter-revolution, and the nature of loyalty and disaffection which these circumstances may induce in individuals. It would really need an original mind to read all these possibilities of sociological knowledge in Durkheim's study of suicide, let alone develop them in any credible way. Weber, in fact, provides incontrovertible proof of the logical independence of sociological analysis and explanation—which philosophers as well as psychological reductionists would do well to look into, before crystallizing their thoughts on the nature of sociological inquiry—without rhetorical declarations one way or the other. It also becomes clear that sociological explanations are concerned with what is assumed in psychological analysis. They are, therefore, fundamental to psychological inquiry, and further, in reality, complementary. Thus, the division between psychological and sociological analyses is not of Chinese boxes but of aspects of explanation based on a clear distinction between what has to be assumed substantively in a particular explanation and what has to be analysed.

This clear distinction between the aspects of explanation of what are, in fact, primarily mental facts and their interpretations —i.e. the assimilation and expression of beliefs, either rational or non-rational—is what enables Weber to be analytical. If he were to give them even a pseudo-concreteness they would be similar to what one finds in Durkheim and his followers. The similarity which a number of writers, since Talcott Parsons's *The Structure of Social Action*, have found between the ideas of Durkheim and Weber is based on such a pseudo-concreteness of concepts; but what has not occurred to them is that *anyone* considering the nature of social reality would, and indeed, must, *identify* what needs to be explained: therefore, it could hardly be surprising that they should deal with the same ideas. The fact that has been ignored is that all the important sociologists have dealt with the same range of ideas, with more or less success. The success or failure of their explanations, therefore, is totally unrelated to the concepts and similarity in the meaning of the definitions or their implications, but it is the way in which their generalized explanations are to be judged true. The explanation is inevitably about the relationship between their concepts and the object of explanation: the relationship which puts to test their whole theoretical and empirical analysis. The congratulation that one thinks is deserved in discovering such a coincidence is without significance: what one has to judge is the exactness of definition in relation to the object of explanation, and, more important, the way in which the relations of the elements of the object, i.e. in its constitution as well as in its formation, are explained. It is exactly to this kind of explanation that Weber's sociological analyses have contributed, and the failure to realize this has been the bane of much of contemporary sociological thinking.

What is, one may ask at this point, Weber's sociology? If it is similar to Durkheim and many others in substance, it is original in, first, correctly defining the nature of action: that means-and-end relationship of reasoning gives the structure of action. Action, in this sense, is the logical term for what in many circumstances may be called 'conduct'. It is impossible to use the term 'behaviour' in Weber's sociology, except as a fragment of conduct or action, for the primary principle of all Weber's analyses is to investigate and not simply to correlate. The difference between investigation and correlation is profound in Weber, because in investigation the establishment of observable correlations is only a preliminary step of analysis. In many cases, it is already given. The recognition of a correlation can be intuitive or studied. In itself it is an accidental coincidence which needs to be causally analysed. In his criticism of intuitionism[4] this point is clearly brought out in the distinction between experience and knowledge, and how intuitionists mistake one for the other. Similarly, the studied correlation of 'empirical' sociological studies is in fact dependent entirely on the validity of the assumed cause, which, at best, is only a hypothetical cause. The hypothesis may be a justified inference on the basis of experience—even in terms of a conceptual scheme or theory—but it can be readily seen that neither a conceptual scheme nor the experience on which it is based turns it into a valid explanation or a knowledge of the cause of the particular correlation. The second step, therefore, is causal analysis to demonstrate that the assumed cause is the real cause. This is the part which Weber's theory of causal analysis or, rather, his methodology is concerned with. The distinction between hypothesis, establishment of correlation and the justification of the hypothesis—or simply between experience and knowledge—is a crucial one in Weber's sociology. For him, such correlations would only be an early part of the casual analysis and in no way the end of sociological knowledge. It is this principle of his methodology which makes sense of the ideal type as a descriptive form. It is constructed after a correlation is established or known. It also shows how the correlative studies have contributed little to a definite knowledge of social reality on their own. It takes us back to the theoretical contributions which an analysis must make to be of any significance.

What then are the theoretical ideas of Weber? The most fundamental idea—which is central to his definition of sociology—is interpretative understanding of social action. Social action, as has been said earlier, is not divorced from individual action : which can only be explained in terms of the actor's psychology, but where the actor has to orientate himself to another. Orientation is an important means of understanding for Weber : it gives the context of action and makes it specific and unique. It is the means by which one is able to translate the specific, the unique, into the general and predictable : this is the means-end relationship of his methodology in concrete situations. The term 'orientation to another' contains the whole of human social experience, but one orientates in different ways to different situations. This fact is generalizable from the explanation of an individual action to the historical—from the historical to the sociological. The logic of Weber's theoretical framework is contained in this completely consistent application of the primary concept of action to the whole range of human experience. Weber rightly believed in a complete consistency between his theory and material researches.[5] Although his work shows an undifferentiated concept of understanding as knowledge, it refers to the meaning of an action in a specific context and, in so far as one understands it intellectually or emotionally, such understanding is knowledge. This kind of understanding, however, is ultimately referable to one's subjective conviction of its truth, but the process of being convinced is what objective knowledge is about. Emotional understanding is not sociologically problematic : it refers to re-experience or sympathy which cannot be demonstrated analytically. Therefore, the phenomenological emphasis on inter-experience of sympathy is in fact irrelevant to sociological analysis. Intellectual understanding is what, in effect, Weber's sociology is concerned with. If it were concerned with sympathetic understanding the whole of his sociology would be a 'reconstruction' of the world—picturesque perhaps, but personal. It can be, and has been, read as such, but Weber's personal vision of the world is not his work's enduring quality. It is precisely because it transcends the privacy of his thoughts that it endures. This transcendence, therefore, is the expression of his intellectual precision.

One is able to judge this precision by intellectual standards, whether they are applied to his theoretical definitions or to his analyses of historical materials, or to the empirical generalizations on the formation of the modern world. The first test through such standards is inevitably on the unity of his methodological position and material researches.

The framework of action, understanding through meaning of action, and the contents of experience from which an action is inevitably derived are the stuff of Weber's sociology. 'How are they related?' is not a question of personal interpretation, but of analytical test. No individual can judge the truth of all that he says, from his personal experience, but everyone can test the validity of his theory, methodology, and empirical analysis. One can first examine the progression of his theoretical ideas, its influences and its implications, but would they give one a conclusive proof of the unity or disunity of his work? They can, if one makes a comparative study of the ideas in relation to the author's aim. Is an author's aim ever clearly postulated at the hour of his first taking up the pen? The problem becomes, therefore, that of the clarification of the author's aim and purpose, and the judgment of his degree of achievement. Thus a critical study of his significance, in his own terms, would reveal the inner contradictions of his ideas and arguments—or the inner consistency. It can also show the quality of thought and experience: the canons of literary criticism, in the end, depend for their value on the discernment of the critic. One can, while agreeing on the quality, read into the argument or the idea certain characteristics which may not be there. It is also difficult to trace influences of others on a piece of writing, but it is a necessary clarification inasmuch as the original contribution of the author lies in seeing new implications and connections of ideas already present in other writings. This is particularly true of Weber—indeed of all analytical writing.

Thus, the test of significance, of unity of thought and accuracy of empirical reference is completed neither by relating the arguments and ideas to the author's life nor with a literary analysis. Sociological thought and analysis cannot depend entirely on the author's philosophical vision or literary gifts. They may only provide the impulse to write, to express his ideas, and give a peculiar form to his works. They may certainly infuse an imaginative urgency in his insights; but they cannot by themselves dictate the accuracy of the contents of his thought and knowledge. This is the point of Weber's distinction between value-judgment and value-relevance. The difference may seem subtle, but it is unambiguous. All judgments are not value-judgments, even though the premise of description may be a value. The logical or empirical judgment when it is confused with a value-judgment because one cannot see the implicit connections with the original ideas, would seem to be a value-judgment. This has happened frequently with Weber's thesis on the Protestant ethic and the spirit of capitalism. His conclusions have been related to his Protestantism, asceticism and the pessimistic nature of his political views. It has also been read, on the other hand, as a sanctification of the capitalist system. It is in the peculiar nature of social facts and their formation that one is unable to differentiate easily between the evaluative statements of the analyst and the logical conclusions of the analysis. The values inherent in the social facts seem very much the same as the values their analyst may be attributed. After all, he chose to study the problem, therefore he must be regarded as sharing the values of the participants. This form of argument fits in completely with a descriptive framework, as objections, either way, are answered through the pseudo-concreteness of classifications. The value-position of the analyst, it is said, is in one category and the value-relevance in another; or it is claimed that they are the same. But one must remember that Weber was not at all concerned with inventing descriptive categories.[6] Analytically, the principle of value-relevance made the same rigorous conditions for the expression of the value-position of the analyst as for the values given in the context of the situation to be investigated. The difference was not made because, analytically, the case of the analyst when he wished to investigate the implications of a value-position he himself held would be no different from the case when he wished to investigate the implications of a value-position he was indifferent to. For, the procedure he would employ in both cases to arrive at an objective conclusion on the implications of any value would be exactly the same. Therefore, the results will be judged in exactly the same manner. Those who believe that declaring one's value-position automatically makes the rest of the analysis objective would seem to have a faith in the unconscious objectivity of the human mind. If value-judgment is a distortion of truth, then the distortion can happen in situations one is not involved in either sympathetically or unsympathetically as well. Indifference may itself be taken as, or become, a distorting factor. The objectivity of analysis and explanation therefore has little to do with explicitness or implicitness or even lack of a value-position.

The characteristics of an empirical judgment on value-facts are fully demonstrated in Weberian sociological analyses. One may ask : how can one judge the empirical significance of ethical orientations and attitudes, which Weber's work is all about? Especially, if one cannot include his personal vision of the world or his literary qualities in making the judgment, and if the line dividing value-judgments and value-relevant interpretations has been so difficult to draw in much of sociological writing. The judgment in fact can be made by a simple separation of form and substance. The form of explanation includes the validation of substantive assumptions, arguments and the relation between description and explanation. These questions may seem entirely philosophical and outside the realm of sociological theory, but these 'philosophical' questions cannot possibly be answered by philosophical analysis, which is necessarily a deductive process. The validity of any substantive assumption can only depend on the accuracy of its general description. No general description of an object is possible without a knowledge of its characteristics. Therefore, the pre-condition of validation of an assumption is, paradoxically, an analysis of its characteristics. Secondly, arguments may seem to depend for their validity entirely on their logical connection with the assumption. Since the assumption itself has to be validated through an analysis of the characteristics of the object, it seems the whole philosophical problem of valid knowledge rests on the accuracy of empirical analysis. How are we to judge this accuracy? This is what Weber's fundamental distinction between meaningful and causal explanation is concerned with. Meaningful explanation is what we have to judge empirically. It is not enough for explanations to mean something.

The meaning, the implication, the relationship between its significance and the resulting experience, or a possibility of experience, must be explained. Explanation means that one can give a correct reason for these connections: one must be able to generalize, infer other possible connections: in short, predict the future course of events, actions in similar contexts. It is obvious that prediction is only possible if one knows the principal cause of the formation of *an* event or action. The principal cause of formation of social events or actions is not an empirical general law of human behaviour. It may be of a metaphysical order, but there is no experiential way, except an intuitive conviction, of determining what it is. Any assertion of a general law of human behaviour is an attempt at a metaphysical explanation-a point which is inherent in Weber's work and has not been realized by earlier philosophical sociologists; nor has it been taken by today's.

What do the contents of Weber's sociology then have which traditional descriptive sociology lacks? First, a theory of sociological knowledge. The discussion of action as a primary unit of analysis is the fundamental formulation of this theory. The second constituent of this theory of sociological knowledge is his definitions of the varieties of social action—the systematics. The third constituent is the analysis of the meanings of action, and the fourth constituent is the body of empirical generalizations on the formation of the modern world. The last part is a direct link with his original personal interest in the sociological sources of modern industrialism, but these empirical generalizations are, for us, substantive theories for comparative study of the non-industrial world: both historical and contemporary. The point about value-judgment and empirical judgment develops a sharpness in this part of Weber's contribution, which we would not have been aware of otherwise. Sociology has always taken the values of Western society as the norm of comparison, and if other developments of this traditional norm led to value-judgment, why does not Weber's? The reason for this is that Weber's definition of the sociological sources of modern society is not a priori, but the conclusion of his analysis—based on a constant comparative perspective, and on an analytical and sociological definition of the notion of rationality itself: a clear distinction between rational and sentimental action. If his substantive analysis is concerned with the rationalization of the world, it is not confined to a particular case of rationalization. The means-end relationship inherent in rationality of action is the framework of analysis—not the content of the action which he is analysing. The content is distinguishable accurately only when it is compared and contrasted with the contents of other forms of rationality. The definition of the substance of Chinese, Indian and Ancient Judaic rational conduct is not arrived at by superimposing the rational conduct of modern Western orientation. The framework allows a proper comparison, a clear generalizable definition, but the substantive analysis tests the framework. No other theory of historical or social sciences has achieved this clear and consistent formulation of a norm of comparison.

The definitions of various social actions through their interrelations and inherent principles are an achievement which is inseparable from this substantial analysis. They can be used separately, precisely because the empirical sociological knowledge which Weber's work gives us makes them general and independent of a specific context. These definitions, however, are not laws of human conduct because they have not been adequately tested in application. They provide the kind of theoretical structure which Parsons and others before him have been attempting to provide, and have quite rightly made important for sociological investigations.

For example, in the discussion of authority and domination—which is perhaps one of the most widely used of Weber's theoretical formulations—Weber writes:

> It is an induction from experience that no system of
> authority voluntarily limits itself to the appeal to material
> or affectual or ideal motives as a basis for guaranteeing its
> continuance. In addition every such system attempts to
> establish and to cultivate the belief in its legitimacy . . . .
> Hence it is useful to classify the types of authority according
> to the kind of claim to legitimacy typically made by each.

And further, 'The choice of this rather than some other basis of classification can only be justified by its result.'[7]

There is in this quotation enough indication of the importance of 'induction from experience' in the classification of types of action for Weber. Further, the way in which he argued the *basis* of his definitions differs fundamentally from the practice of both those who criticize them as being inadequate for their purposes

and those who develop 'typologies' of their own as 'improvements'
on Weber.

Weber's definition of bureaucracy, for example, has been made
the basis of hypothetical extensions of what may be—or, perhaps,
should be, in the author's view—the functions or the practices of
a bureaucracy, because this form of administrative organization is
an immediately recognizable characteristic of modern Western
societies. This kind of 'concrete' thinking has made nonsense of
Weber's precise definitions, which provide a framework for
identifying—and not for containing as the typologists would have
it—actual bureaucracies (through a predominance of the
characteristics distinguished in the pure type over others to be
found in them) in order to understand the effects, causes and contexts of organized authority in society in general, through analysis
—it must be remembered in any reference to Weber—of the
exercise of authority and power in individual societies.[8] It is
obvious that however accurately one generalizes the description
of a particular case, it will not allow us to explain all that is
involved in a Weberian question. One will not even begin to
answer the question if the typological exercise has nothing to base
itself on but the pure thoughts of an a priori theorist.

The important point of such definitions in Weber's work is that
they clarify both the various aspects of modern Western civilization, which was the specific object of his study, and the forms of
social, economic and political organization in general—in terms of
the individual's orientation to these forms. One cannot but see that
the fundamental implication of such a theoretical framework is
that the knowledge of social reality can no longer be a matter of
conjecture, intuition or philosophical belief, but simply of analysis
through an application of certain explicit principles. It should,
however, be remembered that the orientation of the individual to
the forms of organization in a society is invariably ethical:[9] a
principle which is much more empirical as well as comprehensive
than the deterministic clichés of coercion, function, class-conscious-
ness or ideology. It relates the two major principles of Weber's
methodology with empirical reality: value-relevance and means-
end relationship.

There is, however, no assumption of empirical generalization in
these definitions: they are, logically, preliminary and hypothetical,
even if they are, in fact, based on Weber's detailed knowledge and

explicit analysis of a major part of the constituents of modern Western civilization. Their accuracy, therefore, is to be *accepted* on the validity of his empirical analysis—and not either by attributing an intuitive sociological insight to him or by subscribing to the notion that hypothesis necessarily implies explanation : both characteristics being strictly contemporary and non-Weberian in sociological thought.

The comparative studies of major world civilizations also form the inevitable background of the connection between history, economics and sociology in Weber's work. The relation between history (including economic history) and sociology in Weber's work is often confused with the autonomy of narrative history and sociography. In the development of Weber's work, sociography comes as the first step in the analysis of sociological factors, which needs, as a second step, a clarification of historical causes, because all social facts (actions, events and processes) are embedded in history. The analysis of historical, i.e. specific, causes, needs ideal-typical formulations in order to create an experimental framework, without which no causal imputation is possible. The resultant generalization is necessarily both a theory of history and an empirical statement. It is inevitable that a sociological theory should thus replace a conjectural theory of history, as the knowledge of the social and historical processes becomes more accurate. The historical narrative, like sociographical and ethnographical description, provides the raw material of sociological analysis. The misunderstanding, based on comparing the narratives of history with sociographical descriptions, really should not have been projected on to the relationship between sociological theory and the conjectural theories of history, which, incidentally, is also extensible to the relationship of the methodological principles of social scientific knowledge and philosophies of history—with the same inevitable result of replacement. This consequence, however much it may create disturbances in the sentiments of historians and some sociologists, is obvious and inevitable if Weber's work is properly understood and developed. In Weber's work the relation between economics and sociology seems much more straightforward. It is an 'attempt to define certain concepts which are frequently used, and to analyse certain of the simplest sociological relationships in the economic sphere'[10]. However, the same method of means-end characterization is employed in his definitions of 'economic' and 'economically rational' and 'economically oriented' action. That economic action is not a 'psychic' phenomenon nor necessarily a social action is a point which is entirely consistent with the primary definition of action. In the 'modes of orientation of action'[11] the ethical nature of the individual's orientation, even in the economic sphere, is clearly present,[12] but for Weber economic rationality, being 'oriented, by deliberate planning, to economic ends'[13] did not involve the kind of value-interpretation which was necessary for social action. Thus, economic action, being mostly end-oriented rather than value-oriented, was nearer to the pure ideal type and had the rationality of the definitional concepts. In other words, economic action, like the definitional concepts, was immediately understandable, without taking the variety of individual points of view as a point of departure. But, although there is a theoretical similarity in the definitional concepts of economics and sociology, the empirical analysis of economic action involves only the forms appropriate to the end-rational action. Because of the theoretical affinity between economics and sociology it has, in contemporary derivations, been assumed that economic theory is the prototype of sociological theory. The affinity arises because the same formal characteristics have to be applied to both economic and social action, but the limited empirical applicability of the sociological concepts to economic action is decisive in the independence of sociology from economics. Further, since Weber's work has demonstrated that economic ends are neither autonomous nor 'psychic' but subject to metaphysical and social values, it would be impossible to argue convincingly that the principles of economic theory provide any kind of norm for sociological analysis. There is a further point which makes this contention of economically-oriented sociologists or economists with views on sociology even more dubious, that of the inadequacy of economic explanations or theories to account for non-industrialized economies, because of their dogmatic adherence to certain substantive assumptions, on which their theories are based, as formal principles of analysis.

What Weber has shown in his analysis of economic and social organizations is not a substantive coincidence between economic and social action, but the similarity and difference in the nature of concepts to be employed in the analysis of end-rational economic action, and value-rational social action. The analysis of value-determined rational social action is Weber's most original empirical contribution to sociology, with a methodology which is ultimately concerned with the problems of such an analysis without being restricted by the limits of that category of action. Analysis of value-determined non-rational action is possible without modifying his methodology: it becomes simply an extension of the analysis of action to the analysis of values and their formation; although we have in Pareto's theoretical system a working out of a complementary methodology and analytical framework of action and its subjective interpretation.[14]

The papers which follow are arranged in a sequence of themes—theory, relevance of values, methodology, empirical thesis on the relations of historical, economic and religious facts, and approach to the problems of sociography—which designate the boundaries of Weber's sociology as a whole. This sequence may seem to be a reversal of the general development of his inquiries,[15] but, for an introductory critique, it is necessary because any judgment of the significance of his contribution to sociological knowledge must begin with a general discussion and provide a context to the reference and meaning of particular statements.

All the papers are independent contributions to the understanding of Weber, in the sense that they are expressions of the individual author's special interest and approach. Yet they form, because of the critical independence, an unusually coherent tribute, arising mainly from the authors' sense of inquiry rather than categorization of Weber in the history of sociological literature. Those who would condemn Weber to be an object of ancestor worship, as one of the 'founding fathers', must be unaware of the timelessness of intellectual expression. Without a critical conscience about one's debt to past thinkers, one's trivial thoughts begin to sparkle with the glitter of originality and grit of self-admiration. One has, without it, no standards by which to judge one's own experience or to recognize the quality of one's thought.

Notes:

1   Such as the excellent précis in R. Bendix, *Max Weber: An Intellectual Portrait*, Anchor Books, New York, 1962; Methuen, London, 1966.

2   Cf. 'The present work departs from Simmel's method (in the *Soziologie* and the *Philosophie des Geldes*) in drawing a sharp distinction between subjectively intended and objectively valid "meanings"; two different things which Simmel not only fails to

distinguish but often deliberately treats as belonging together':
M. Weber, *The Theory of Social and Economic Organization*, Free
Press paperback edition, 1964, p. 88.

3 E. Durkheim, *The Rules of Sociological Method*, Free Press paperback edition, 1966, p. 2.

4 Cf. Talcott Parsons, *The Structure of Social Action*, Free Press
paperback edition, vol. II, p. 587 nn. 3 and 4. Parsons, in fact, falls
into the same confusion as the intuitionists, when he says that
'experience itself is never "raw" but is itself "in terms of a conceptual scheme" '. The conceptual scheme of an experience which
is to be analysed is certainly not the conceptual scheme of its
explanation.

5 Cf. A. von Schelting, *Max Webers Wissenschaftslehre*, J. C. B.
Mohr (Paul Siebeck), Tübingen, 1934, p. 362. In von Schelting's view,
Weber's material work breaks through his methodological limits
on the notion of understanding. In fact, both Weber's consistent
theoretical and methodological ideas and the evidence of his
empirical analyses make for a delimitation of understanding as
knowledge.

6 A point which becomes increasingly clear simply by reading Parsons's criticism of Weber, made over and over again, that he did
not go far enough in a priori theorizing. A study of Weber's
sociology as a whole leaves one with no justification for Parsons's
criticism, as Weber did not at any stage consider that sociology
could be a priori: how can *interpretative* understanding ever be a
priori? If it were *intuitive* understanding, then Parsons would be
a greater sociological theorist than Weber.

7 Weber, *Theory of Social and Economic Organization*, op.cit., p. 325.

8 Cf. *ibid.*, pp. 109–12.

9 Cf. *ibid,.* p. 129: 'From a sociological point of view an "ethical"
standard is one to which men attribute a certain type of value
and which, by virtue of this belief, they treat as a valid norm
governing their action.'

10 *Ibid.*, p. 158.

11 *Ibid.*, pp. 166–7.

12 Cf. *ibid.*, p. 166 (including editor's n.9): 'The development of
rational economic action . . . has been to a large extent determined by non-economic events and action, including those outside everyday routine and also by the pressure of necessity . . .'

13 *Ibid.*, p. 158.

14 Cf. my Hindu Reformist Ethics and the Weber Thesis: An
Application of Max Weber's Methodology, 2 vols, London
University Ph.D. thesis (unpublished), 1969, for a discussion of the
comprehensiveness of Weber and Pareto in the substantive sense,
as well as in their formal concepts mentioned below in my paper.

15 Cf. E. Baumgarten, *Max Weber: Werk und Person*, J. C. B. Mohr
(Paul Siebeck), Tübingen, 1964, *Zeittafel*, pp. 681–720.

Two

John Rex

Typology and objectivity: A comment on Weber's four sociological methods

Sociology is the discipline which seeks to understand and explain the working of structures of social relations and social inter-action. Given the nature of its subject matter it would seem prima facie to be unlikely that it could assimilate its methodology to that of the natural sciences except in the most general sense. But the problem goes beyond this. It is that hitherto *both* natural and non-natural science methodological models have failed to describe what the best sociological studies actually do. For the most part the natural science models simply fail to do justice to the epistemological complexity of the sociologist's interaction with his subject matter. What is less often realized, however, is that the most important non-natural science models miss the main issue and tend to trivialize the sociologist's task.

The work of Max Weber serves as a useful reference point for any discussion of the methodological options open to the sociologist. In his work, as it developed over a period of thirty years, four alternative lines of thought were explored. It will be convenient to signpost these as representing the influence exer-cized over Weber successively by Rickert, by Dilthey, by posi-tivism and by Georg Simmel. Our object in this paper, however, is not to reopen all the issues involved in the great and scholarly debates about methodology in which Weber joined. It is simply to show that the four lines of thought all survive in contemporary sociology and still have great significance for us. More specifically, however, it will be argued that in practice it was Weber's fourth method which was most important for him, that this method is important today, and that its importance has been obscured by the concentration of Weberian scholarship on the other three. The method is that which is used in Weber's comparative and historical studies, which leads to the formulation of concepts of social structure, and which gives some social and political relevance to the sociology of social forms which Simmel had the genius to propose but which he also failed to apply adequately.

The notion of ideal types is the methodological notion most frequently associated with the name of Weber. But, as it is usually formulated, it appears to have little relationship to the way in which what are later called ideal types are actually used in Weber's *Wirtschaft und Gesellschaft*. It is important therefore to distinguish this notion from the structural emphasis of the later work. Too often the work of Weber is praised or dismissed as though it rested solely on the earlier methodological doctrine.

The first formulation of the notion of ideal types arises in the course of Weber's thinking as an economic historian and at a time when he was still to some considerable degree under the influence of Rickert. It emphasizes the dissimilarity between ideal types and laws, the interests of the investigator in particular rather than in general problems, and the relevance in sociological research of value-standpoints. It is a concept which creates the greatest possible gap between what Weber saw himself as doing and what is normally understood as science. But it also described, and this is far less commonly understood, an approach to history very far removed indeed from that which Weber used in his later comparative studies.

Our aim is to distinguish Weber's final method from that suggested in his earlier essays and to that end we shall show how his early position created difficulties for him, how he sought to resolve these difficulties by moving towards an alternative position, which at the same time solved the problem of the relation of *verstehen* to positivist science, and how finally he abandoned his early notion of ideal types altogether.

It is a curious fact that what should often be taken as Weber's definitive position on the methodology of sociology was one which he did not advocate in the context of sociology at all, but rather as the appropriate method for the economic historian. True, he confuses matters somewhat by writing of the 'science' of the concrete individual instance, but for all this his early essay on 'Objectivity in social science'[1] starts by accepting Rickert's distinction between history on the one hand and all sciences, natural and social on the other. Ideal types are therefore seen essentially as the tool of the historian. The aim of the essay on objectivity is to describe the logic of their use and to show the differences as well as the similarities between this use and that of laws in the natural sciences.

Weber's starting point is that of 'relevance for value'. He arrives at this by a rather circuitous route, showing, first, that, contrary to Simmel's view, there is no purely social sphere, but that all social phenomena are social from a particular point of view, i.e. they may be relevant economically, politically, religiously and so on. The question then becomes one of asking whether such one-sided starting points make objectivity in history impossible. Weber's answer to this question is that they do not, but that none the less the actual logical status of the tools used by the historian is quite different from that of the tools of the scientist.

Weber's argument is that, although the historian may use value-relevant starting points, he does not by virtue of that fact, have to be unobjective. There is a clear enough reason for this. No claim is made by Weber (as distinct from Rickert) that these value starting points themselves have an objective validity. They are seen as having been chosen from an infinite number of possible starting points and no suggestion is made that they have anything more than conditional status. Thus the proposition we are invited to accept takes the form 'If you want to achieve X, you must do Y' and we *can* accept it without being required to accept the subjectively chosen value standpoint of the historian who put it forward.

More important than this, however, is Weber's insistence that the causal link between a desired state of affairs and what has to be done to achieve it can be objectively demonstrated. The significance of ideal types is that they are essentially propositions which assert these causal links. Thus, once we make our value starting points explicit, true objectivity becomes possible. For Weber, as for Myrdal, in his classic appendix on facts and valuations in social science,[2] we attain objectivity by declaring our value standpoints. Subjectivity in a bad sense is the result of suppressing the fact that we have such standpoints. Unfortunately, however, in drawing the sharp distinction which he does between the value starting point and the subsequent causal proof which he does, Weber arrives at a conception of the logical status of ideal types which is, to say the least of it, arguable.

A great deal depends here upon the analysis of causality adopted. For those who share the present writer's view it is in fact difficult to maintain Weber's notion of objective causal demonstration without making some reference to law-like statements of a general kind and there is evidence to suggest that at a later point Weber came to accept this. At this point, however, he insisted upon the methodological distinctiveness of the ideal type, with the result that the very definition of the notion is marked by certain peculiar features.

Our view of causality may be briefly stated as follows: to say that A causes B is to say that B has always followed A in observed cases *and that it has done so necessarily*. The real problem in the analysis of causality, however, is to say what the nature of this necessity is. Our answer would be that the necessity lies in the deducibility of the statement 'B follows A' from some general proposition which we accept as true. Thus, according to this analysis, the use of causal terms involves an implicit reference to general propositions. It is of course possible to avoid using causal statements but, if they are used, the acceptance of general laws, theories or models becomes inescapable.

Had Weber argued that the choice of value starting points did not make sociology or history unobjective because these value starting points led to causal investigations, and that these causal investigations in turn rested upon testable general propositions, no difficulty would have arisen. In insisting that his ideal types do not refer to such general laws, however, he raises doubts as to whether his causal investigations as well as the initial value standpoints are objective. In Weber's view, it would appear, the necessity of observed connections between events is to be demonstrated with the aid of ideal types which refer to unique historical situations. The trouble with this is that it is difficult to see what such types can add to simple descriptions if they are so concrete and particular in their reference. Weber is therefore forced into arguing that while they refer to objectively possible cases, they involve 'an artificial accentuation of certain elements of reality'. It is not easy to see how such artificial accentuations of reality can be said to have any objective validity. At most they come to be regarded as 'yardsticks', but the choice of relevant yardsticks seems to be as much a matter of subjective choice as is the choice of initial value-standpoints.

Clearly another option would have been open to Weber had he not still been so much under the influence of Rickert and had he been writing about sociology rather than about economic history. This was that ideal types referred to pure cases, not in some special sense, but in the same sense as scientific laws did, and that actual cases occurring in non-experimental circumstances could be explained by using a number of ideal types in combination. Thus in so far as our first ideal type did not explain reality we would not necessarily be compelled to reject it, but before we could claim that it was still relevant to the case under consideration we would have to introduce other ideal types to explain the empirical residue. If, for example, the ideal type of economic man did not fully explain the exchange behaviour of a rural community we should still be able to say that the type had some relevance if we could explain the deviation from the ideal in terms of some other pure type (e.g. a model of a system of kinship obligations). This alternative, however, is explicitly rejected by Weber in his early essay.

It should now be noted, however, that the early essay does not assume the existence of subjectively formulated concepts. What he says about ideal types might apply to any social science concepts whether formulated from the standpoint of a hypothetical actor or not. The essay was written before he entered the controversy opened up by Dilthey's discussion of *verstehen* as the appropriate method of the social sciences. But when he does begin to discuss social facts in this new way, a *twofold* change occurs. Not merely do ideal types refer to ideal or pure types of motivation or action-orientation, they are also apparently regarded as propositions testable in terms of their predictive power rather than mere yardsticks against which empirical reality can be measured. Thus the central problem in relating the essay on 'Objectivity in social science' to the opening chapter of *Wirtschaft und Gesellschaft* is to understand what Weber meant by explanations which are adequate on the level of meaning and explanations which are casually adequate.

The notions of meaning and cause were both implicit in Weber's early essay and he saw them as compatible with each other. Probably, however, this was simply because he had not completely distinguished the two concepts. Very often the relationships which he was considering were relations of meaning (e.g. the relationship between Protestantism and the spirit of capitalism) and his attempt to treat them as causal relations was only possible given an unclear conception of causality. In *Wirtschaft und Gesellschaft*, however, Weber actually attempts to define the two notions and the difference between them comes out into the open.

Dilthey had distinguished between natural science which looks for laws and causes, and the human studies which look for relations of meaning. As he put it, 'The uniformities which can be established in the field of society are in numbers, importance and precision, far behind the laws which it has been possible to lay down for nature on the sure foundation of relations in space and time.'[3] And Weber in 1904 would probably have agreed with this. As he wrote then, 'Meaningfulness naturally does not coincide with laws as such and the more general the law the less the coincidence.'[4]

In the opening chapter of *Wirtschaft und Gesellschaft*,[5] however, we are confronted with the following:

> The interpretation of a coherent course of conduct is 'subjectively adequate' or adequate on the level of meaning insofar as, according to our habitual modes of thought and feeling, its component parts taken in their mutual relation are recognized to constitute a typical complex of meaning.
>
> The interpretation of a sequence of events will on the other hand be causally adequate insofar as, according to established generalization from experience, there is a probability that it will always occur in the same way.
>
> If adequacy on the level of meaning is lacking, then, no matter how high the degree of uniformity and how precisely its probability can be numerically determined, it is still an incomprehensible statistical probability, whether we deal with overt or subjective processes. On the other hand even the most perfect adequacy on the level of meaning has causal significance from a sociological point of view only if there is some kind of proof for the existence of a probability that action in fact normally takes the course which has been held to be meaningful. For this there must be some degree of determinable frequency of approximation to an average or pure type.

It would seem from this (1) that Weber now equates ideal types with meaningfully adequate explanations, but (2) regards them as incomplete unless the course of action which they hold to be meaningful actually has a probability of occurrence. What is interesting about this is that the relation between meaningfully adequate explanation and the actually observed event is different from that which existed between the ideal type and empirical reality in the earlier essay. Apparently it is now possible to talk of 'proof' of what is held to be meaningful in ideal typical terms.

Not surprisingly Weber's attempt to bridge the gap between *verstehen* and probabilistic and positivistic explanations has been attacked from both sides. He has been criticized by philosophers[6] and by the phenomenological school in modern sociology[7] for having attempted to scientize the concept of meaning and by the positivists[8] for having hung on to unprovable metaphysical concepts. Thus some draw the lesson that what is required is a philosophic discipline which can distinguish rule-governed action from other forms of behaviour, some that more attention should be given to the actor's definition of the situation, while others argue that Weber pointed the way, even if he did not follow it, to the operationalization and quantification of sociological concepts.

In fact Weber seems to have made things unnecessarily difficult for himself. For to say that explanations on the level of meaning can become more than merely plausible theories, or to say that they are in some sense subject to proof, is not to say that proof must be provided in the sense of a statement of statistical probability such as he suggests. For surely an explanation in terms of meaning implies that there will be certain distinctly observable behavioural events occurring together and this *is* subject to proof. Moreover it is in the nature of an explanation in terms of meaning that it suggests other behavioural events which might be observed, apart from those which first led to the formulation of a meaningful hypothesis. Thus it is not simply the recurrence of one simple behaviour sequence which provides proof and verification, but a whole range and variety of relevant events.

Those who have suggested that mere statements of statistical frequency add nothing to meaningful explanations have probably taken Weber too literally. It is quite true that the mere fact that the man cutting wood always cuts wood at a particular time of day adds nothing to our interpretation of his behaviour as meaningful. But, if there are alternative explanations in terms of meaning, clearly there are other aspects of his behaviour which will provide confirmation that one interpretation rather than another is true. In this sense the logic of *verstehen* is not all that far removed from that of empirical science. Both involve the elaboration and testing of hypotheses.

But to say this of the logic of *verstehen* is not to say it about ideal types, more particularly about ideal types in the sense in which Weber first defined them. What we have here is a confusion of the two separate discussions about *verstehen* and science (the debate with Dilthey) and the debate about value-relevance and ideal types in history. Neither debate is clarified by the confusion. Weber does want to insist that *verstehen* is not incompatible with verification and in the course of developing this argument he talks about pure or ideal types of action orientation. But ideal types in this sense have little to do with ideal types which involve an artificial accentuation of certain aspects of reality in order to point to particular causal sequences.

The debate about *verstehen* and science, however, is confused in itself. Weber seems to have gone too far in trying to meet the claims of positive science and hence landed himself in a position far less easily defensible than would have been the case had he stuck to arguing that there was some relationship between the logic of *verstehen* and the logic of scientific proof. What he does is to try to relate *verstehen* to a specific kind of scientific proof based upon the demonstration of probabilities of a statistically determinable kind. This might have had the effect of giving sociology a certain respectability in scientific circles, but in the event the position was untenable and most of Weber's successors have therefore been forced to abandon either his concern with meaning or his tendencies towards scientific positivism. Neither of these positions does Weber justice and what is overlooked is that the whole argument about the two types of explanation is intended to lead into a discussion about truly sociological concepts (i.e. concepts which refer not merely to the meaning of action but to social relations and structures of social relations). In the course of this latter discussion Weber develops his fourth method which is distinct from both the phenomenological and the positivist methods which are commonly attributed to him on the basis of the opening pages of *Wirtschaft und Gesellschaft*.

The use of positivistic language in Weber's discussion of causally adequate explanations and of social relationships has led to his being given a certain guarded recognition by modern positivism despite what would appear to those who write in this tradition to be an unfortunate concern with history and with meaning. Thus, for example, Lazarsfeld and Oberschall draw an entirely positivist lesson from Weber's opening chapter: [9]

> Weber . . . recognized the probabilistic nature of indicators and he expressed this in sociological concepts. Passages like the following occur frequently:
> 'It is only the existence of the probability that a certain type of action will take place that constitutes the "existence" of a friendship. Thus that a friendship exists or has existed means only this: that we, the observers, judge that there is or has been a probability that on the basis of known subjective attitudes of certain individuals there will result in an average sense a certain specific type of action.'
> Weber specifically stresses that only in such probabilistic terms can the meaning of social relationships be caught. They cease to exist, he says, whenever there is no longer a probability that certain kinds of meaningfully oriented social action will take place.

Thus Weber can be read as doing what Durkheim did in his *Rules of Sociological Method*, namely starting with a definition of the social which started from the subjective point of view of the participant actor (that which is 'capable of exercizing over the individual an external constraint') but, because of the difficulty involved in using this concept in empirical work, replacing it with another (that which defines the social as that 'which is general throughout a given society, while at the same time existing in its own right independent of its individual manifestations').[10] But, while Durkheimian sociology is normally recognized as having developed in the direction of quantitative statistical work, the Lazarsfeld and Oberschall view of Weber is noteworthy for how much of the contrary evidence in Weber's own writing it ignores.

The opposite lesson can also be drawn from Weber. It is not that he pointed the way to ahistorical and meaningless work of a positivist kind but that, in failing to establish the compatibility between the two kinds of explanation, as he claimed, he pointed to the necessity of confining sociology to the study of meaning, with all the complexity that that concept involves.

It may have been noted that Weber uses meaning in two different senses in his early essay and in *Wirtschaft und Gesellschaft*. In the essay he is concerned with the 'significance of a configuration of cultural phenomena'.[11] In *Wirtschaft und Gesellschaft* he is concerned above all with the meaning of behaviour in one specific context, namely that of purposive action. In arguing that hypotheses about the meaning of action could be subjected to some kind of empirical test Weber seems to have been referring to meaning in this second sense.

What Schutz and his pupils have done is to insist that the notion of meaning cannot be confined in this way. They may allow that one form of meaning is that which is involved when an actor fantasies a state of affairs which he wishes to bring into being and then develops a project for the attainment of that state of affairs. But no such state of affairs and no such project can be envisaged until the actor already lives in a meaningful world. Thus the essential prolegomenon to all sociology is a sociology of knowledge, which is taken to mean an account of their subjective definition of their situations by participant actors whom the sociologist observes. Sometimes, indeed, sociology comes to be identified with the phenomenology of everyday life.[12]

Phenomenological sociology with this kind of emphasis now forms a powerful minority movement within contemporary sociology and has begun to formulate its own methods of research in opposition to those of positivism. But the phenomenological emphasis upon subjective meaning divorced from verification procedures of a broadly scientific sort loses much of what was essential to Weber's approach. It fails to recognize that Weber was not solely concerned with the actor's own subjective meaning attributed to his situation, but with the meaning of the situation for a constructed hypothetical actor. And it fails to recognize that Weber was primarily concerned with the effect on human behaviour not merely of meaning but of meaningful social relations. Thus one danger is that phenomenology might trivialize sociology and never establish that kind of explanatory purchase on empirical reality which Weber so notably achieved.

We do not need, however, to take a stand either for phenomenology or for the positivistic study of behaviour. Both have their uses and Weber was aware of them. The important thing, however, is that Weber went on from his initial argument about the relationship between *verstehen* and natural science to argue for a more complex sociological method altogether, which only arguably depended upon his having bridged the gap between the *Naturwissenschaften* and the *Geisteswissenschaften*.

It is too often forgotten that the whole of the discussion in the early part of the first chapter of *Wirtschaft und Gesellschaft* is only preparatory to Weber's discussion of social relationships. True, he does define sociology as concerned with the interpretation of social action, but what follows is a discussion of complexes of social relations. It is this that forms the substance of Weber's work, and which, through its focus on structure, distinguishes Weber sharply from those of his successors in the phenomenological school who appear to be interested only in subjective meaning or the actor's definition of the situation. It is this too that makes it possible for Weber not to trivialize sociology and to concern himself with the major questions of social and economic history.

It would have been possible for Weber to have approached this discussion of social relationships in a quite different way, and, had he done so, he could have avoided much of the controversy surrounding his use of the term *verstehen*. The difficulties relating to the verification of his structural hypotheses then would probably not have been raised in so sharp a form. (Any more in fact than they have been in the case of the work of Durkheim, even though the relationship between his 'methodologically collectivist hypotheses, and empirical fact is not one whit less problematic than that between Weber's subjectively formulated hypotheses and observed probabilities in the empirical world.)

The really important point to notice about Weber's concept of social relationships is simply that he defines it in such a way as to avoid reification. This can be seen by contrasting it with Durkheim's concept of social facts. Whereas the latter are described as external to the individual, and not merely to one individual treated as 'ego' for the purposes of analysis, but external to all individuals and, therefore, unexplained 'things', Weber's social relationships refer to the orientation of the action of one actor to the action of another. Far from being reified external things, therefore, they refer to subjectively understandable courses of action. The other actor in the social relationship may appear as external to ego, but he is no supra-individual thing.

Marx, it may be noted, was on the same side as Weber in this issue, at least in his early writings. In discussing his notion of alienation he raises the question of the nature of the social object which confronts man as an alien being or thing and concludes:[13]

> The alien being to whom labour and the produce of labour belongs, in whose service labour is done, and for whose benefit the produce of labour is provided, can only be man himself.
>
> If the product of the labour does not belong to the worker, if it confronts him as an alien power, this can only be because it belongs to some other man than the worker.

Clearly Marx here shares Weber's opposition to the reification of sociological concepts. Moreover this impression is reinforced in his most interesting attempt to formulate sociological concepts——the *Theses on Feuerbach*, in which he explicitly contrasts his own dialectical materialism with that current in his day, by saying that his starting point is not something external to man but human activity itself.[14]

Weber's opposition to the reification of social, relational and group concepts has been labelled methodological individualism. This is reasonable enough. Discussions about methodological individualism, however, have sometimes been taken to mean that the concepts which Weber uses stand or fall by his success or failure in showing that explanations adequate on the level of meaning have the exact relationship to causally adequate explanations which he attributed to them. In fact, however, all that is assumed in the later discussion is that hypotheses about actors' motivation, which are taken for granted in the concepts referring to social relations, do not need to remain as mere plausible stories. They are in principle testable, and those which have relevance to a particular piece of observed behaviour may be distinguished from those which do not.

But, with this said, it should also be noticed that Weber did not believe that every reference to a social relationship should be justified by a complete proof of the relevance of the hypotheses offered for the action orientation of each of the participant actors. The possibility of such proof remains in the background, but the model of a social relationship would in any case suggest its own verifiers. These might refer to sequences of behaviour hypothesized in types of action orientation but it might also refer to behaviour, events and things, which arise, not so much in action, as in inter- action. If then the main task of sociology is seen as the delineation of the principle kinds of social relations, groups, institutions and structures, it should be possible to indicate what sorts of evidence should be required, before one could say that a particular relation, group, institution or structure existed. Perhaps it might be argued that the verification of such statements which is possible is imper- fect, because all possible falsifiers or verifiers have not been con- sidered, but this would be equally true in the case of many of the constructs of physical science and it would certainly be some- thing to be expected in the case of complex entities like social relations. The great merit of Max Weber was that he tried to achieve as exact definitions and proof of sociological concepts and propositions as was possible without abandoning the actual problems with which sociology was faced.

Before leaving the topic of Weber's opposition to the reification of concepts there is one other fundamental point to notice. This concerns the key role of the concept of legitimate order in the transition which occurs in his chapter from the discussion of action to the discussion of social relationships. If a social relationship is not to be left to rest simply upon an incomprehensible statistical probability there must be some other ground for suggesting that alter will fulfil ego's expectation. This other ground Weber finds *in a subjective belief* on the part of the two parties that they are subject to a legitimate order. Thus Weber does not admit the reification of the notion of norms any more than he does the reification of the notion of social relations. All human society is for him something which rests upon human motivation, action orientation and choice. It has no ontological validity beyond this. This is not to say, of course, that, once certain subjective attitudes and orientations exist, their existence does not produce unintended consequences. But it is to say that social facts can be changed and manipulated by human beings if they start in the right place.

In the transition from talking about action and *verstehen* to talking about social relations, however, there is another change of perspective on Weber's part which is of first importance. Indeed it is probably the most crucial in the development of his sociology as a whole. This is that Weber no longer concentrates on the *content* of human action as it appears in the actor's subjective understanding. What Weber actually talks about are the *forms* of social life. This raises the whole question of the relationship of his work with that of Simmel, and, even more important, whether the justification of the sorts of concepts and propositions which Weber put forward might not be looked for, not where we have been looking for it and where Weber himself looked for it, in a methodology acceptable to positivist science, but in the kind of neo-Kantian and phenomenological approach which Simmel's work suggests.

Weber, it will be remembered, specifically rejected Simmel's notion of formal sociology in his essay 'Objectivity in Social Science'. As he puts it there,[16]

> the term 'social' which seems to have a quite general meaning, turns out to have, as soon as one carefully examines its application, a particular specifically coloured though often indefinite meaning. Its generality rests on nothing but its ambiguity. It provides, when taken in its 'general meaning', no specific point of view from which the significance of given elements of culture can be analysed.

Moreover the notion of *verstehen* itself would appear to rest upon a concern for the content rather than the form of social action.

Yet when we turn to *Wirtschaft und Gesellschaft*, once the initial controversy with Dilthey has been set on one side, we find Weber talking about the social forms separated from their content in precisely the way which Simmel advocated. Indeed some of the actual topics chosen for analysis are precisely those which had first been opened up by Simmel. What Weber seems to have discovered is that the orientation of the actor to another depends primarily upon the formal aspects of action and of the relationship with the other. Thus without going into all the concrete uniqueness of history there is a great deal that the sociologist can do in constructing models of the main forms of social relations and group structure.

Weber, of course, did not arrive at this conclusion by constructing a series of sociological atoms and building from them. He started by believing that the concrete particularity and cultural uniqueness of something like the Protestant ethic was the sociological topic par excellence. But as he pursued his sociological studies he began to see that whether one was studying religion, administration, urban life or economic and productive organization, what went on in one society was comparable, even though it might be sharply different from, what went on in another. And it was possible because the number of possible forms of social action is not infinitely variable. Having discovered this in the course of his historical studies, Weber went back to the elements in *Wirtschaft und Gesellschaft* and sought to give system to the concepts which he had previously developed ad hoc in his historical studies. This is something which he would have had to do even if his argument with Dilthey had never occurred. The types of action which lie behind the process of *verstehen* are not designed simply to interpret the social or other action of particular actors. They are the building blocks from which the whole edifice of Weber's theory is constructed.

Tenbruck has argued in a penetrating essay[16] on Simmel's formal concepts that Weber and Simmel were engaged in the same enterprise. But it is possible that he confuses the issue by suggesting that Simmel's forms are akin to Weber's ideal types. For, although ideal types do by definition involve selecting from the whole of the observable world only a limited number of observations, these observations need not be of a formal kind. Indeed it was one of Weber's early contentions about ideal types that they should not be. But the interesting point about the later work is that he not merely insists upon the constructed nature of his concepts, but that he *also* finds it profitable to select out *formal* aspects of social action and relationships for study.

What are these formal aspects and how are they arrived at? This is probably the most important question that the methodology of sociology has to face if sociologists are to clarify what is, to put it no higher, the most important of their methods. Unfortunately neither Simmel nor Weber really succeeded in doing this. Simmel believed that while the method which we use in practice was clear enough, its elucidation at the moment was only possible by way of analogy,[17] while Weber seems to lose the important methodological discussion about the social forms in a quite different discussion about ideal types and about *verstehen*.

Tenbruck rightly points out that the interpretation of Simmel which holds that he is concerned with lifeless forms in abstraction from content is unjust. Simmel always held that it was only in particular historical circumstances that they could be observed. Equally Weber arrived at the forms only as a result of wide-ranging historical studies and after a long discussion of meaning. But what then are the formal aspects of social relations which are abstracted from the meaningful content of history?

One misleading view which is enjoying a certain current vogue is that which merges the study of social facts with the study of culture and language and sets as its goal the discovery of deep structures of an abstract kind underlying all of these spheres. This may have its uses, but what is noticeable about this kind of 'structuralism' is that it does not take into account the subjective meaning of a situation for an actor. Nor does it explicitly distinguish social from other forms of structure.

Weber's approach first of all distinguishes the field of action from other fields of investigation and then, within action, concentrates on action which in 'its subjective meaning takes account of the behaviour of others and is thereby oriented in its course'. Now we can, of course, take account of the content as distinct from the forms of the behaviour of others and this may be one important area of study within the total field of social interaction. But there are two further points to be made here. One is that, when we compare cases of interaction which have widely differing contents, we discover that there are recurrent underlying forms. The other is that the actors themselves sometimes orient their conduct not to what alter does but to the form of what he does.

Can one say more about the forms than this? Is there a definition of social form as opposed to content? Probably there is no such definition on an abstract level. We define the forms when we give them a systematic exposition as Weber did. This, however, still leaves open the question of how Simmel or Weber could have arrived at such a systematic exposition. This is a question which Weber never really faces and to which Simmel gives only the ghost of an answer in his controversial essay 'How is society possible?'[18]

Simmel's essay suggests the analogy with the Kantian question 'How is nature possible?' and leads to the conclusion that in interpreting the manifold of observed human behaviour as social we impose on it certain social categories. If this were the case we should have a sociology a priori[19] concerned not with empirical investigation but with elucidating the interrelationships between formal concepts. Alternatively, if we allow for the greater complexity of sociological, as compared with natural scientific investigation which arises from the facts that not merely sociological observers but the actors observed have and use sociological concepts, we might be inclined to embark upon an empirical search for the categories through the study of the actor's definition of his formal situation.

For our part we would reject both the notion of a sociology a priori and the sort of phenomenological empiricism which looks only at the actor's own definition of his situation. We reject the first because there do not appear to be any given social categories in the same way as the Kantian categories may be thought of as given, and we reject the second because we find in practice that we have no direct and immediate access to the subjective meaning of his situation as it appears to the actor himself. The truth of the matter lies between these extremes and it emerges in the way in which Weber himself proceeded.

The first stage of Weber's comparative and historical investigation was one in which he sought to describe the social systems he was dealing with in language as close as possible to that used by the actors themselves. Such descriptions, however, could never exactly describe the social meanings as the actors themselves saw them. They were at best, approximations, and involved some abstraction from the full particularity of any given situation. What is much more important, however, is what happens at the second stage. This is that, given the existence of sociological accounts of a variety of different social systems, historians and sociologists who have access to more than one account, in a way that participant actors do not, find that it is possible to translate the language of the particular accounts into a common language and to agree amongst themselves on the description in this new language of any particular social system. What we have, therefore, is not simply a single language and a single set of categories, known to us a priori, nor, on the other hand, an infinite variety of different categories and an infinite number of languages. What we find is that it is possible to develop an agreed sociological language and a limited number of agreed categories which appear to explain, not just this or that particular situation or social system, but all the major historical social systems.

As sociologist and historian Weber might well have rested his methodological case there, and for most practical purposes what has been said above is all that needs to be said. After all, it is possible to make historical statements about social structures without defining every term in terms of the observable behaviour of ulti- mate individual actors. But Weber did also attempt to go further. He tried to reduce the language of comparative sociology to its action elements and, in the course of so doing, did actually try to operationalize the concepts which he had used so that the way in which they could be ultimately tested could be established at least in principle.

This third stage in the development of formal sociological concepts may well be the main task of sociological theory and certainly Weber's discussion of fundamental concepts in this way ranks among the two or three major contributions to sociological theory. It is unfortunate, however, that in seeking to systematize his concepts in this way he appeared to make his comparative and historical method dependent upon more particular propositions about *verstehen* and about positive science.

What we have sought to show in this paper, then, may be summarized as follows. During the course of his career Weber approached sociological problems at several different levels. At the outset he was concerned with the study of particular cultures and historical periods and developed the notion of the ideal type as the specific method of cultural social and historical analysis. Secondly he turned his attention to the epistemological questions raised by Dilthey in his discussion of *verstehen*. This led him to a close analysis of the notion of 'subjective meaning for an actor' on the one hand and the methods of quantitative empirical science on the other. Weber thought that he could bridge the gap between these two and hence seemed to give his support both to an empirical phenomenological and to a positivistic sociological tradition. All three of these discussions, however, were essentially preliminary to what became his overriding interest, namely the comparative study of the major historical social systems. For that purpose he was forced into the business of elaborating a systematic formal socio- logical language in terms of which comparisons could be made bet- ween one sociological system and another. It was the elaboration of that language and its formal sociological concepts which constituted Weber's most lasting contribution to sociology.

One thing which is not helpful to the understanding of this last phase of Weber's is the use of the term 'ideal types' to refer to his structural concepts. There is a sense, of course, to which all scientific concepts and theories are ideal types and if this were meant no great harm would be done by using the term. Why it is misleading in the case of Weber's work is that he himself had used it, first, in a very special sense to refer to value-relevant concepts involved in elucidating particular complexes of meaning, and, second, in distinguishing between subjective meaning for the observed actor himself and meanings imputed by an observer during the process of *verstehen*. The structural concepts which Weber finally put forward are not subject to the difficulties to which these more particular notions of ideal type are subject and the aim of this chapter has been to show that whatever the difficulties raised by his three earlier methodological concerns, Weber's fourth method still stands in its own right. Its significance is likely to be overlooked in the contemporary sociological world where the only options on offer often appear to be those of positivism and empirical phenomenology.

Notes:

1 'Objectivity in social science and social policy', in Weber, *The Methodology of the Social Sciences*, Free Press, Chicago, 1949, pp. 49–112.
2 G. Myrdal, *Value in Social Theory*, Routledge & Kegan Paul, 1958, pp. 119–65.
3 H. A. Hodges, *Wilhelm Dilthey. An Introduction*, Routledge & Kegan Paul, 1949, p. 145.
4 Weber, *Methodology*, pp. 76–7.
5 Weber, *Economy and Society*, Bedminster Press, New York, 1968, pp. 11–12.
6 P. Winch, *The Idea of a Social Science*, Routledge & Kegan Paul.
7 A. Schutz, *The Phenomenology of the Social World*, North Western University Press, 1967.
8 See P. Lazarsfeld and A. Oberschall, 'Max Weber and empirical social research', *American Sociological Review*, vol. 30, no. 2, April 1965, pp. 185–98, for a positivist interpretation of Weber's work.
9 Op cit., p. 193.
10 E. Durkheim, *The Rules of Sociological Method*, Free Press, Chicago, 1938, p. 13.
11 Weber, *Methodology*, p. 76.
12 For the development of Schutz's work see especially A. Schutz, *Collected Papers*, vol. 1, M. Nijhoff, The Hague, 1967, introduction by M. Natanson, pp. XXV–XLVII; P. Berger and T. Luckman, *The Social Construction of Reality*, Allen Lane, 1967; H. Garfinkel, *Studies in Ethnomethodology*, Prentice-Hall, New Jersey, 1967.

13 K. Marx, *Economy and Philosophical Manuscripts of 1844*, Foreign Languages Publishing House, Moscow, 1959, p. 79.
14 K. Marx and F. Engels, *Selected Works*, vol. II, Foreign Languages Publishing House, Moscow, p. 403.
15 Weber, *Methodology*, p. 68.
16 K. H. Wolff (ed.), *Georg Simmel, 1858-1918*, Ohio State University Press, pp. 61-99.
17 *Ibid.*, p. 64.
18 In *ibid.*, pp. 337-56.
19 For the most explicit interpretation of Simmel in this direction see D. Martindale, *The Nature and Types of Sociological Theory*, Routledge & Kegan Paul, 1961, p. 236-46.

Three

Alan Dawe   **The relevance of values**

So much has already been said about Max Weber's discussion of the relationship between social science and value that it is almost impossible not to wonder, with Professor Aron, whether it is 'possible to say anything essentially new about Weber's value theory'.[1] However, I take comfort in the fact that novelty is more often a function of relevance to new movements of thought and action than it is the result of originality. For I want to suggest that it is the present situation in which sociology and sociologists find themselves that gives renewed relevance to what Weber had to say about the role of values in sociological analysis and research. For many years, it has not even been possible to ask the questions he asked with any prospect of arousing serious interest. They have been smothered, though not answered, by a sociological consensus centred on structural-functionalism and located within the positivistic intellectual world that has defined the limits of our knowledge of human society for so long.

There has been little room for Weber in this particular world. Most of what has been written and said about his value theory has been regarded as peripheral to the real work of contemporary sociology. His impact on the modern sociological consciousness has been limited to that gross misconception of his thought which represents him as the arch-priest of value-neutrality. Now, however, there are signs that the consensus of recent years is breaking down. Not only in sociology, but in most fields of thought concerned with the understanding of social interaction, people are beginning to break away and follow new paths: notably, in the last year or so, into applications of phenomenological theories of knowledge to sociological and psychological analysis. As yet, in terms of their impact on dominant modes of thought, these movements are small. Moreover, they are by no means as new as some of their proponents appear to believe. For one thing, they are often as much motivated by the age-old obsession with the scientific status of social science as were the most positivistic of the founding fathers; hence the extreme formalism of much neo-phenomenological social analysis. For another, they cannot so easily ignore the obvious continuities between their work and that of the major figures in the history of social thought. It is from these continuities—from, for example, the links between the work of Weber on meaning and the neo-phenomenological attempt to recover for sociology the sensitivity to meaning—that the new movements will derive whatever enduring value they may turn out to have. Otherwise they will degenerate into short-lived fashion.

I doubt, however, whether they can be dismissed as mere fashion, however much their more intoxicated disciples may tempt one to do so. For they have brought back to the very centre of sociology questions about methodology, meaning and significance, about which we have been silent for too long. In so doing, they represent and express a 'rupture' within the positivist and functionalist consensus;[2] that is, 'a radical break with the whole pattern and frame of reference of the existing notions in an ideological field' which prefaces the 'construction of a new pattern'.[3] Substitute 'sociological' for 'ideological' and one begins to see the significance of schools of thought which produce, for example, such stark and explicit oppositions as that between Durkheim and Jack Douglas on suicide.[4] Or which lead—albeit indirectly, but in a field many will regard as being closer to the everyday work of modern sociology—to the equally significant contrast between the dominant behaviourism of mass media studies and the recent Leicester study of the intricate process whereby the media translate events into 'news' by the a priori attribution to them of established meanings and values.[5]

But all this amounts to much more than a mere break in modes of thought and analysis. The whole history of sociology shows that it has always been shaped and defined by the social and moral preoccupations of its time and place. At this particular time, the rupture in sociological discourse coincides with the increasing breakdown of social and political consensus in precisely those societies where the sociological consensus has been most dominant. This cannot be—however dangerous it may be to draw connections between phenomena of the present—mere coincidence. For it is impossible to gainsay the vast and widening gulf between a sociology of consensus and a social and political reality characterized by such deep divisions and polarizations that concepts like 'structural differentiation', 'tension-management' and 'role-strain' become totally inadequate as explanatory tools. When such a gap appears, it is inevitable that people will begin to question not merely the sociological frameworks of which these concepts are a part, but their basic ideological and epistemological assumptions. Not only the functionalist framework, but also the positivist view of knowledge, value and the relationship between the two becomes problematic. In a word, new movements of thought in sociology have a political and, beyond that, an ethical dimension. They remind us again of something that, in the presumption of scientific detachment, we had forgotten. They remind us that sociology, like all forms of intellectual activity, derives its concepts, propositions, theories and methods from its context of value.

This, however, is no new lesson. In essence, it is the lesson that, in the situation of sociology and its practitioners today, we have to learn from Weber. Not that one would think so, in view of the way Weber's value theory has been represented hitherto. Indeed, one would think the opposite. For modern sociology, despite all that has been said about its complexity, that theory has become a simple justification for value-neutrality; for the radical separation of fact and value, social science and moral concern. 'Science is concerned with questions of fact. Propositions about values—prescriptive propositions—are logically distinct from descriptive propositions'.[6] This is the simplistic message modern sociology has perceived in Weber's immense and many-sided attempt *to bridge the gulf between science and value*. We may accept that values will play some part in the selection of problems for investigation. But, conveniently, the selection of problems is relegated to a pre-scientific stage of inquiry. The real business of science is the construction and testing—particularly the testing—of hypotheses, and this process can and must be value-free. Only if we ignore the vast bulk of what Weber said on the subject can we find any warrant in his writings for this interpretation.

There may seem to be greater justification for drawing from his work a sociology of means; that is, for representing him as defining sociological propositions in terms of the formula, 'if you want to achieve X, you must do Y', where, though the proposition itself is conditional upon the value X, *our acceptance of it* is not dependent upon our acceptance of that value, but only upon a strictly neutral judgment about the scientific adequacy of the relationship between ends and means.[7] But even here, the invitation is still to strict value-neutrality. We may be asked to declare our values, but only so that we may then get on with the real job of sociology. Once again, values end where science begins.

Weber's value theory

This is not to say that these interpretations do not express any aspects of Weber's value theory. The meaning of this, for example, is clear and unequivocal: 'It can never be the task of an empirical science to provide binding norms and ideals from which directives for immediate practical activity can be derived'.[8] But this proposition conveys, for Weber, only one feature of the relationship between science and value. Indeed, it provides only the starting point for his discussion of that relationship:[9]

> When we distinguished in principle between 'value-judgments' and 'empirical knowledge', we presupposed the existence of an unconditionally valid type of knowledge in the social sciences, i.e., the analytical ordering of empirical reality. This presupposition now becomes our problem in the sense that we must discuss the meaning of objectively 'valid' truth in the social sciences.

And it is with this problematic in the relationship between social science and value that Weber's central arguments begin. It is only now that he moves to the real substance of his discussion—the substance that modern sociology has chosen to ignore, but which is again, in our present situation, supremely relevant. It is well worth recalling this part of Weber's argument, if only to remind ourselves of its complexity:[10]

> 'Culture' is a finite segment of the meaningless infinity of the world process, a segment on which human beings confer meaning and significance . . . . The transcendental presupposition of every cultural science lies . . . in the fact that we are cultural beings, endowed with the capacity and the will to take a deliberate attitude towards the world and to lend it significance. Whatever this significance may be, it will lead us to judge certain phenomena of human

existence in its light and to respond to them as being (positively or negatively) meaningful. Whatever may be the content of this attitude, these phenomena have cultural significance for us and on this significance alone rests its scientific interest.

It follows that[11]

The concept of culture is a value-concept. Empirical reality becomes 'culture' to us because and insofar as we relate it to value ideas. It includes those segments and only those segments of reality which have become significant to us because of this value-relevance. Only a small portion of existing concrete reality is coloured by our value-conditioned interest and it alone is significant to us. It is significant because it reveals relationships which are important to us due to their connection with our values.

Accordingly[12]

All knowledge of cultural reality, as may be seen, is always knowledge from particular points of view . . . without the investigator's evaluative ideas, there would be no principle of selection of subject-matter and no meaningful knowledge of the concrete reality . . . And the values to which the scientific genius relates the object of enquiry may determine, i.e., decide the 'conception' of a whole epoch.

Moreover, 'in the method of investigation, the guiding "point of view" is of great importance for the construction of the conceptual scheme which will be used in the investigation.'[13] All of which leads to an inevitable conclusion :[14]

There is no absolutely 'objective' scientific analysis of culture—or . . . of 'social phenomena' independent of special and 'one-sided' viewpoints according to which— expressly or tacitly, consciously or unconsciously—they are selected, analyzed and organised for expository purposes.

Granted, this is only part of the argument. Granted that Weber goes on to discuss how, given the basis of value upon which social science inevitably rests, we may none the less attain objectivity through the construction of ideal types and the test of causal adequacy. But in what he has already said, there is much more than the simple formulae we have drawn from him about the role of values in sociological inquiry. There is much more than a simple point about not providing norms for practical activity; much more, too, than an attenuated proposal that sociological propositions must take the form, 'if you want to achieve X, you must do Y.'

Indeed, an interpretation almost diametrically opposed to these is suggested by the Weberian prescriptions quoted here. For they testify to the fact that Weber is arguing for the centrality of value to social science, not merely as a 'principle of selection of subject-matter', but *as the sine qua non of all meaningful knowledge of social reality*. Without the attribution of value, knowledge of social phenomena is inconceivable. We impose value on concrete reality. We define social phenomena and the relationships between them in terms of our 'value-conditioned interest'. It is only on the basis of our 'one-sided viewpoints' that social phenomena are 'selected, analyzed and organised for expository purposes'. Our 'evaluative ideas' decide the 'conception of whole epochs'. In sum, the point is precisely that our concepts, our propositions, our theories and our view of methodology all derive their meaning from the attribution of value.

The role of value in Weber's sociology

The extent to which this is so can be seen from Weber's own work, for his sociology is demonstrably rooted in and permeated by his moral vision. His ethical world is that of autonomous individual choice from an infinity of possible values. In other words, he maintains an uncompromising individualist ethic, but one far removed from the sentimental and socially antiquated liberalism usually associated with moral individualism. For Weber's is a bleak world, where moral choice faces morally isolated individuals, not so much as an ideal, but as a continuous, necessary and frightening fact of the human condition. It is the wilderness of the Judean prophet, the eternally threatening abyss of the demon-ridden Puritan, the constant purgatory of the Protestant entrepreneur, perpetually fearful of damnation. It is a polytheistic world in which each of us must, because we cannot do otherwise, choose our own 'god or demon'. Each of us must impose our own meaning upon an otherwise meaningless world. And the process of so doing is a process of unceasing struggle, not only against meaninglessness and chaos, but also against the meanings others are likewise struggling to impose on the world: 'The highest ideals, which move us most forcefully, are always formed only in the struggle with other ideals which are just as sacred to others as ours are to us.'[15] And he imported this chilling ethic into his sociological vision; indeed, the last quotation comes, not from one of his political speeches or from a tangential comment on ethics, but from his central essay on methodology. No wonder he saw his sociology as a test of 'how much I can endure'.[16]

The connections between his ethic and his sociology are not hard to see. His whole conception of the nature of the discipline rests upon his view of the world as consisting of autonomous individuals, choosing from an infinity of values and struggling to impose their own meanings upon their existence. This is the world the sociologist faces and of which he has to make sociological sense. But he, too, is part of this world. Hence Weber's conception of empirical reality as a meaningless chaos upon which the sociologist, like his subjects, has to confer meaning; his conception of culture as a 'finite segment' of meaningless infinity on which 'human beings confer meaning and significance'; of the sociological task as being the understanding of those finite segments of meaning and the relationships between them; of the selection, analysis and organization of 'social phenomena' according to the 'one-sided viewpoint'; and from all this, the supreme significance of 'relevance to value' as the pre-condition of all knowledge of the empirical social world.

The line from the ethical position to the methodological position is clear and undeviating. So, too, is the line from the same basic values to the formal categories in terms of which Weber defines sociology. Certainly, as Professor Rex has shown, there is a decisive shift in his work from his early concentration on ideal types to his later emphasis on structural categories.[17] But these categories are still defined in terms of meaning; in other words, the attribution of value is still the basis of sociological analysis. Thus the subject-matter of sociology is 'social action' and 'action is "social" insofar as its subjective meaning takes account of the behaviour of others and is thereby oriented in its course.'[18] Social action, therefore, is still about the struggle between meanings in the world. The social relationship, the real core of Weber's sociology, still turns on meaning; the meaningful relationships between actors in a plurality. And when he goes on to define formally the many types of plurality, it is always in terms of the types of meaning upon which they rest. Weber sums up the whole conception himself, even at the late structural stage of his work, with the following:[19]

> For sociological purposes there is no such thing as a collective personality which 'acts'. When reference is made in a sociological context to a state, a nation, a corporation, a family or an army corps, what is meant is, on the contrary, *only* a certain kind of development of actual or possible social actions of individual persons.

Again, the individualist creation of meaning central to his ethical world is mirrored in his sociology. But even now, the line is not yet fully drawn. For Weber's ethic, having been reproduced in his view of methodology and in his formal categories, finally becomes the basis of his substantive work.

To take a central example: since his sociology of domination stands at the very centre of his work, domination is clearly the prime social relationship in Weber's view. And for him, it turns on legitimacy—the acceptance by one group, on whatever basis, of a meaning imposed on them by another group, which thereby legitimates its dominance. At the same time, legitimacy rests ultimately on the implicit sanction of force. Moreover, it is always precarious (and much of Weber's work is devoted to an analysis of the ways in which it can be maintained, and of the pressures making for its breakdown and mutation into other forms). Once again, the parallel is clear. Once again, the ethical components— the conflict of meanings, the struggle to impose one's own meaning against other meanings and thus on other actors, and the unceasing nature of the whole process—come together at the heart of the sociology.

But there is more than a parallel here. For the fundamental point is that *the sociology is entailed by the ethic*. The decisive notion, evidently, is that of the attribution of value or meaning, central to both Weber's ethical and sociological worlds. It is the foundation of the concepts of subjective meaning and relevance to value, which are the key to the translation from one world to the other. These concepts imply a double confrontation with value. The sociologist confronts the values of those he studies—their struggle to impose meaning and their consequent interaction with the meanings of others. But he also confronts his own values. He, too, must impose meaning and, therefore, negate other meanings. And the consequence of this is that the 'one-sided viewpoint' of social phenomena, defined in terms of value, is rooted in a concept of subjective meaning in which there is a fusion of the values of the sociologist and the value of the actors he studies. Subjective meaning, therefore, does not refer simply to participant values, to actors' definitions of situations; these can never be directly grasped. It stands midway between participant definitions and observer definitions, a crucial intervening variable, conflating elements of the meanings of each. In this sense, the observer becomes a participant, a variable in his own analyses. And there is an obvious connection here between Weber and ethnomethodology, the sociological derivative of neo-phenomenology. For one of the major themes of ethnomethodology is precisely the role of the sociologist as participant. For example, a principal argument of Cicourel is that the attribution of meaning by the sociologist becomes a decisive qualitative variable intervening between social phenomena and their measurements.[20]

The implication of this point, however, goes far beyond methodology, ethno- or otherwise. In that his own values enter his sociology in the complex and specific way denoted by the concept of subjective meaning, the sociologist does not only select problems on the basis of those values, nor does he merely analyse and organize social phenomena in terms of them. *He also propagates them.* This is not simply something he should do, another exhortation of the 'sociology on trial' type. It is something he cannot avoid doing. It is inherent in the very nature of his work as a sociologist, in the very process of analysing and communicating subjective meanings, of which his own values are inescapably a part.

Weber and the problem of control

The wider significance of this process, both for Weber's own sociology and for its relevance to the contemporary sociological situation, becomes very clear when we look more closely at the values which shaped that sociology and which, therefore, it propagated. To reiterate the basic point, Weber's preoccupation, both ethically and sociologically, is with the attribution of meaning: more specifically, with the imposition of meaning upon the various situations faced in the world and therefore upon other actors in those situations. And this preoccupation is the hallmark of one of the central problems of sociology. One of these central problems is the familiar problem of order. The other, which expresses this concern with the attribution and imposition of meaning, is what I have called elsewhere *the problem of control*.[21]

Briefly, the problem of control—born, as far as sociology is concerned, of the Enlightenment—refers to an enduring theme in Western social thought: the concern with the problem of regaining human control over essentially man-made social institutions and historical situations, through the human construction and imposition of ideal meanings. It involves a view of social man as the creator of society, a view diametrically opposed to that implicit in the problem of order, which conceives of social man as the derivative of society. It is obviously a social philosophy or, in Aron's term, a 'doctrine' and, as such, communicates an ethical imperative.[22] But it communicates it through sociology. Specifically, it generates a sociology of social action (in opposition to the sociology of social system derived from the problem of order), in which the actor is conceived of as interacting with others on the basis of his attempt to control their action in order to impose his own meanings or definitions upon situations involving both himself and others. Hence the familiar language of action, founded on the premises of subjectivity and historicity, and involving the notions of ends, means, conditions and selective standards. Hence, too, the picture of the social system as the *resultant* of the interaction, defined in terms of relationships of control, between its participants.[23]

That the problem of control is a central concern for Weber is evident from his concentration on the attribution of meaning, from his categories of social action and from his sociology of domination, which is essentially concerned with relations of control. But this conclusion does not depend on inference alone. Weber himself testified, openly and passionately, to his profound concern with the problem of control, nowhere more powerfully than in his famous speech on bureaucracy as an all-pervasive feature of modern life:[24]

Already now, rational calculation is manifest at every
stage. By it, the performance of each individual worker is
mathematically measured, each man becomes a little cog in
the machine and, aware of this, his one preoccupation is
whether he can become a bigger cog . . . it is horrible to
think that the world could one day be filled with those
little cogs, little men clinging to little jobs and striving
towards bigger ones . . . this passion for bureaucracy is
enough to drive one to despair. It is as if we were deliberately
to become men who need order and nothing but order, who
become nervous and cowardly if for one moment this order
wavers, and helpless if they are torn away from their total
incorporation in it. That the world should know no men
but these; it is in such an evolution that we are already
caught up, and the great question is therefore not how we
can promote and hasten it, but what we can oppose to this
machinery in order to keep a portion of mankind free from
this parcelling-out of the soul, from this supreme mastery
of the bureaucratic way of life.

That is a classic statement of the problem of control; of the sense
that social institutions, initially the creations of human beings,
have become totally compulsive and dominant over them. And
when Weber remarks elsewhere that 'the Puritan wanted to work
in a calling; we are forced to do so',[25] he expresses in a single
sentence the same sense of the transformation of human agency
into human bondage.

The impact on Weber's sociology of his concern with the
problem of control is clear enough. It leads to his life-long interest
in the processes of rationalization and thence to his concept of
rationality. And it leads to those aspects of his sociology to which
I have already referred; in a word, to that view of the discipline
which involves a conception of the social system as the resultant
of social action and interaction. Again, Weber himself sums up
that conception:[26]

In general, for sociology, concepts such as 'state',
'association', 'feudalism' and the like designate certain
categories of human interaction. Hence it is the task of
sociology to reduce these concepts to 'understandable'

action, that is, without exception, to the actions of
participating individual men.

But notice: this must mean the *ethical* task of sociology. For this
edict hardly expresses Weber's view of a society in which 'the
actions of participating individual men' are determined by a compulsive and omniscient bureaucracy. Rather, it expresses his view
of the society that should be, a society in which participating
individuals have recovered control of their own action and of the
institutions created by that action. So, for the sociology, the ethical
basis is indeed decisive. That sociology constitutes an answer to
the problem of control and thus propagates the values inherent in
the concern with that problem.[27]

Weber's own work, then, amply demonstrates the point that
sociological concepts, propositions, theories and methodologies are
ultimately dependent on their context of value. And it is at the level
of value that the most important link between that work and the
rupture in modern sociology emerges. I suggested earlier that the
current rupture has a political dimension. The recurring themes
of the social and political movements which provide its content of
value are, however naïvely they may often be expressed, those of
opposition to 'the system', to the machine; and of participation, of
control over the processes and decisions which shape the lives of
those subject to them. Consider, for example, the following:

> There is a time when the operations of the machine become
> so odious, make you so sick at heart, that you can't take
> part, you can't even tacitly take part. And you've got to
> put your bodies upon the gears and upon the wheels, upon
> the levers, upon all the apparatus, and you've got to make it
> stop. And you've got to indicate to the people who run it, to
> the people who own it, that unless you're free the machine
> will be prevented from working at all.

That was Mario Savio, speaking to the Free Speech Movement at
Berkeley in 1964.[28] And the resemblance between his polemic and
Weber's assault on bureaucracy is striking. To be sure, the two
passages are significantly dissonant—Savio's idiom is less ornate,
more colloquial and closer to the rhetoric of grass-roots politics
than Weber's—in ways that reveal immense differences in social

context and conceptions of political action. Nonetheless, what first draws the attention is the same concern, the same feeling, the same urgency verging on desperation. Weber and Savio, sixty years apart, identify the same fundamental social and political crisis. And they communicate their sense of it through the same imagery: the imagery of machinery.

The current upsurge of militant dissent has produced countless statments of this kind, all of them expressing the same revulsion against the 'machine' and the same thrust towards control. Moreover, these concerns are by no means confined to modern American and Western European societies. They are also central to the Marxist humanism which has recently become prominent in the social thought of Eastern European societies, and which constitutes the basis of revisionist attacks on Marxist orthodoxy and on the monolithic bureaucracy legitimated by that orthodoxy. One thinks of 'socialism with a human face' and immediately the connection between this and the same themes in contemporary Western political thought and action becomes very clear. They occupy the same position in a contemporary polarization that currently unites many spheres and locations of intellectual, cultural, imaginative and, above all, political activity. They are both concerned with and activated by the problem of control; the problem Weber proclaimed, in his polemic against bureaucracy, as the fundamental social and political issue facing modern industrial society (even if his own views about the answers were scarcely radical in political terms). And for sociology, that concern is emerging now as a renewed preoccupation with meaning in such movements as ethnomethodology.

Objectivity, method and the communication of meaning

Again, then, we see a somewhat different Weber from the one we have chosen to follow hitherto. It is a Weber for whom we relevance of value to sociology is paramount; for whom sociology is an evaluating discipline, geared not only to the analysis of value, but—because this is inescapable—to its propagation. But what of the other Weber, who took great pains to distinguish between the ethical imperative and the cultural value, between value-judgment and value-interpretation, in order to distinguish between science and value? How do objectivity and value-neutrality, which Weber undoubtedly did emphasize, fit into a sociology defined by and geared to the attribution of value?

The first point to make here is the simple one that objectivity and value-neutrality do not mean the same thing. Essentially, all that Weber meant by objectivity was that, within the limits of the inescapably one-sided viewpoint, it is both possible and necessary to validate one's substantive propositions. There need, of course, be no argument with this. In any form of discussion, there is obviously an obligation upon us to provide criteria whereby our empirical propositions can be justified in relation to the phenomena to which they refer. This, however, is scarcely the distinctively scientific claim it is usually taken to be; scarcely a proposition which defines sociology as a science and science itself as a distinctive activity. For it is a necessary test of all forms of argument, be they sociological, ethical or whatever, that in so far as they incorporate propositions with an empirical content, those propositions shall be shown, by means of agreed criteria, to connect with the empirical world.

This is not to deny the continuing importance for sociology of the search for such criteria, for the relative lack of them is still a large problem in the discipline. But it is to suggest that we keep this search in perspective. Sociology is not merely a method or a set of techniques. Yet, in our obsession with its scientific status, we have developed a conception of science which reduces it to an allegedly distinctive method. Moreover, given that we conceive of this method in terms of an oversimplified view of natural science, this has meant in effect the reduction of the sociological task to the precise measurement and the mathematical inference. And the simplistic interpretations of Weber mentioned earlier tend to reinforce this conception, since they reduce his value theory to the misconceived claim that our scientific status depends upon finding adequate techniques of verification.

Certainly, he wished to achieve as precise and rigorous a form of proposition as possible. But if we look at the methods he actually used in his collection and treatment of data, we find that he was far from being as inflexible and as blinded by science as we have become. The following, again from one of his essays on methodology, is an eloquent description of the way in which we confront phenomena in order to discover their relations to value:[29]

> Value-interpretation . . . develops and raises to the level of
> explicit 'evaluation' that which we 'feel' dimly and
> vaguely . . . What it actually 'suggests' in the course of
> analysis are rather various possible relationships of the
> object to values. The 'attitude' which the evaluated object
> calls forth in us need not be a positive one . . . for the
> person making it . . . an interpretation can despite its
> negative character, indeed even because of it, provide
> 'knowledge' for him in the sense that it, as we say, extends
> his 'inner life', and his 'mental and spiritual horizon' and
> makes him capable of comprehending and thinking through
> the possibilities and nuances of life-patterns as such . . . or,
> in other words, to make his 'psyche', so to speak, more
> 'sensitive to values'.

There are two points about the method he is describing here which
are extremely important, both for the understanding of his own
work and for the discussion of methods in modern sociology. The
first is that the method he describes constitutes yet another deriva-
tion of the emphasis he places on the attribution of value and,
therefore, of his own value-basis. For it is the method appropriate
to his double confrontation with value. The observer approaches
the object of analysis—whether a document, a literary text or an
interaction situation—with his own values, as he cannot avoid
doing. But he must also be open and responsive to the values
inherent in the object itself.

Secondly, and consequently, what Weber is talking about here
is the sensitivity of the empathetic historian to the levels of meaning carried by his objects of analysis. It is also the sensitivity of
the literary critic in the English 'culture and society' tradition, the
sensitivity born of the practice of close textual reading. Indeed,
Weber makes this point himself when he goes on to suggest that
'the interpretation of the textual-linguistic "meaning" of a literary
object and the interpretation of . . . meaning in this value-oriented
sense of the word may in fact proceed hand in hand, ever so
frequently and with good reason.'[30] More than this, he applied the
method in question in his most famous substantive work and, in
the process, demonstrated its immense potential for sociology.
With an acute sensitivity to the 'possibilities and nuances of life-
patterns', he built from a localized literary product—the writings

of Benjamin Franklin—the vast, generalized concept of 'the spirit of capitalism'.[31] And the way in which, in developing his thesis, he moves back and forth between the general concept and the local text provides an object lesson for modern sociologists.[32]

For one thing, it underlines the fact that our concentration on the quantitative, emanating from a narrow view of the nature of scientific method, is stultifying in terms of the search for method itself. It is stultifying in that it closes our eyes to the potential of such methods as those of the historian and the literary critic. It is also stultifying in that it has destroyed the sensitivity of sociologists to levels of meaning and expressions of value these methods demand. Tone, style, feeling, emphasis, inflection, imagery—these are as important to the search for sociological meaning as they are to the understanding of historical meaning and the interpretation of products of the creative imagination. Yet, in their anxious pursuit of scientific respectability, sociologists restrict themselves unnecessarily and inflexibly to what, in comparison with the wide range of potentially fruitful and undeniably relevant methods available to them in principle, is a meagre and stereotyped set of techniques and symbols, from which they can glean only the shallowest messages at the most superficial levels of meaning. Thus is the sociological imagination bequeathed to us by Weber and his contemporaries suppressed. It is especially opportune, therefore, that one product of the current rupture in sociology seems likely to be a long-overdue and liberating recovery of a Weberian flexibility in the exploration of methodological possibilities. Again, the reference is to ethnomethodology, whose central technique is a close reading of interaction situations which, though the objects of analysis are different, has obvious affinities with the close reading of a literary text.[33]

There is, however, a further lesson we have still to learn from Weber's response to value, as exemplified by his treatment of the writings of Franklin and his discussion of the spirit of capitalism. Consider the following passage from that discussion, in which Weber refers to the doctrine of predestination:[34]

> It was this doctrine in its magnificent consistency which, in the fateful epoch of the seventeenth century, upheld the belief of the militant defenders of the holy life that they were weapons in the hand of God, and executors of His

providential will. Moreover, it prevented a premature collapse into a purely utilitarian doctrine of good works in this world which would never have been capable of motivating such tremendous sacrifices for non-rational ideal ends.

Here, Weber is discussing the motivation behind the rational morality of Puritanism which was, for him, so central to the spirit of capitalism. The passage represents, in other words, an integral part of his sociological analysis. But, in the present context, what is striking about it is its tone, which is far removed from the coolly analytical style of modern sociology. It is loaded with the terminology of value and saturated with the vocabulary of feeling. And the point is that the use of evaluative and emotive terms is in no way superfluous or damaging to the analysis. On the contrary, it is essential to what Weber is trying to do. To achieve his analytical purpose, he has to establish not merely the cognitive elements of the meaning of the doctrine in question, but the strength of the motivation behind it. He has to convey what it must have felt like to have believed in this doctrine; to capture the experience of being one of its 'militant defenders'. In short, he has to communicate as many of the levels of meaning involved as it is possible to express by means of the written word. Hence a style designed, not only to present a reasoned and logical argument, but also to spark off, associatively and spontaneously, the feelings and evaluations which are central to the whole analysis. And Weber employs the technique again, even more powerfully, towards the end of the same work:[35]

> Since asceticism undertook to remodel the world and to work out its ideals in the world, material goods have gained an increasing and finally an inexorable power over the lives of men as at no previous period in history. Today the spirit of religious asceticism—whether finally, who knows?—has escaped from the cage. But victorious capitalism, since it rests on mechanical foundations, needs its support no longer. The rosy blush of its laughing heir, the Enlightenment, seems also to be irretrievably fading, and the idea of duty in one's calling prowls about in our lives like the ghost of dead religious beliefs.

Here, Weber compresses, into a few graphic sentences, his view of
the long process of change in the spirit of capitalism between its
genesis and the time at which he was writing. With remarkable
economy, he contrives to summarize the manifold social and cultural processes involved, to indicate the ways in which they inter-
locked and, at the same time, to grasp them at the level of
individual experience. In one phrase, he captures both the carefree
optimism of the Enlightenment and the disillusionment which
later overtook it; in another, both the advance of secularization
and the vague feeling in many lives of guilt and disquiet at the
decline of the sense of calling. And once again, the point is that
both the masterly economy and the immense suggestiveness of the
passage are utterly dependent upon a language laden with value
and evocative of feeling. Once again, without the expressive
characteristics of that language, it would be impossible to communicate the meanings central to Weber's analytical purpose.

In passages such as these, Weber demonstrates a simple point,
yet one that, because of our inhibited responses to value, we have
completely missed. It is that to convey the meaning and value in
which social relationships are rooted, *we have to use the language
of meaning and value.* It is not enough simply to become more
flexible in our use of methods of analysis; these are, in any case,
inseparable from our means of communication. Nor is it enough
simply to make coy confessions of our own values in a preface to
the 'real' job of sociological research, as if they were so much
excess baggage to be declared to the customs officers of scientific
neutrality. We have to allow the whole terminology of value to
permeate our analyses, because that is the only terminology which
can convey the full complexity of meaning. Again, there are
useful examples for us in the best of literary criticism and the
best of history. But we should also look at the major figures in our
own field; at Weber, at Marx, at Durkheim. For their language,
too, is the language of value, not just in polemical asides, but at
the centre of their work, and in their very definitions and classifications. It is Weber, for example, who speaks of 'inner strength and
inner restraint' when defining charisma.[36]

In short, how we *communicate* sociological meaning is an
inextricable part of that meaning; which is to say that our
techniques of communication constitute yet another dimension of
the process whereby we become, through the double confronta-

tion with value, participants in our own analyses. The implication of this is both fundamental and radical. For what is at issue here is the very vocabulary of sociology, and the whole style and tone of sociological writing. Today, we are prevented from exploring and grasping meaning and value because we are not allowed to use its terminology. In our anxiety to avoid any suspicion of contamination by value, we have developed a language incapable of expressing the real complexity and depth of sociological meaning and devoid, even, of the genuine precision claimed as its objective. Once again, the dessicated style of modern sociological writing is totally destructive of sensitivity to the levels of meaning and expressions of value central to the understanding of social phenomena.

In this situation, it is surely time that we recognized the inevitable attribution of value in sociological analysis, not as a limitation, but as a liberation and, indeed, as a prerequisite for the development of the full potential of sociology. Such a recognition would in no way compromise our objectivity, in the proper sense of that term; as should now be clear, it did not compromise Weber's. In fact, to allow value to surface, through our terminology, at every stage of our work can only enhance it. To the extent that our values constitute a variable in our own analyses, we have to declare them and demonstrate their impact on those analyses. Allowing the language of value to permeate our work is a more effective way of doing so than confining it to an introductory statement, which rarely connects and often seems at odds with what follows.

Ethical neutrality and the moral realm

When we come to Weber's more specific doctrine of ethical neutrality, the position is more complex. On the one hand, it is inherent in his sociology that it conveys an ethical imperative. On the other, he clearly denied that sociology could provide such imperatives; we cannot make value-judgments on the basis of empirical science. There is seemingly an element of contradiction in the way Weber explicitly states his position—*but not in the position itself*. For what are at issue in his argument are the grounds upon which value-judgments can be justified. And it is clear that, if sociology is shaped by value, it cannot become the justification for that value; the argument would be entirely circular. In short, to say that value can only be defended within its own universe of discourse in no way rules out the shaping by value of other universes of discourse, and thus the communication of ethical imperatives through them.

In this instance, a logical point for once has real substance, for it demonstrates that what emerges from the doctrine of ethical neutrality is once again the autonomy of the moral realm in Weber's scheme of things. And there is little doubt that the defence of that realm against the encroachment of science mattered at least as much, and almost certainly more, to Weber than the defence of science against value. This is not to say that he was not concerned with scientific integrity. On the contrary, he spoke about it with considerable feeling:[37]

> And whoever lacks the capacity to put on blinders, so to speak, and to come up to the idea that the fate of his soul depends upon whether or not he makes the correct conjecture at this passage of this manuscript may as well stay away from science.

Indeed, the feeling betrays the value; that is Weber choosing one of his own demons. But, time and again, he justified his doctrine of ethical neutrality as a means of preserving, not scientific integrity, but the integrity of the moral realm. There can be no doubt about the meaning of this, for example:[38]

> The reason why I turn on every occasion with extreme bitterness and a certain pedantry against the contaminations of being and duty is not because I undervalue questions of duty, but precisely the contrary, because I do not believe that questions of universal importance . . . can be dealt with like questions of economics or become the object of special disciplines like political economy.

So knowledge alone cannot create meaning:[39]

> The fate of an epoch which has eaten of the tree of knowledge is that it must know that we cannot learn the meaning of the world from the results of its analysis, be it ever so perfect; it must rather be in a position to create this meaning itself.

Least of all can sociology pre-empt the moral realm:[40]

> The social sciences, which are strictly empirical sciences, are the least fitted to presume to save the individual the difficulty of making a choice, and they should therefore not create the impression that they can do so.

In the relationship between science and value, then, the latter is again paramount.[41] But what concerned Weber, and led him to advance his doctrine of ethical neutrality, was his view that social science *was* usurping the moral realm. It *was* creating the impression that it could 'save the individual the difficulty of making a choice'. By incorporating law-like statements of natural right, and by then claiming a purely technical status for social and economic policy recommendations, it was passing off value-judgments as scientific fact:[42]

> When we call to mind the practical problems of economic and social policy (in the usual sense), we see that there are many, indeed countless, practical questions in the discussion of which there seems to be general agreement about the self-evident character of certain goals.

But this is entirely illegitimate, for 'once we pass from the sphere of technical standards, we are face to face with the endless multiplicity of possible evaluations.'[43] Accordingly:[44]

> What we must vigorously oppose is the view that one may be 'scientifically' contented with the conventional self-evidentness of very widely accepted value-judgments. The specific function of science, it seems to me, is just the opposite; namely, to ask questions about these things which convention makes self-evident.

In short, he was bitterly opposed to the dishonesty of dealing with moral and political issues amorally and non-politically; of displacing values with techniques, ends with means. It was the claim to omniscience on the part of social science, both in policy-making and in ethical debate, that he saw as being destructive of the moral realm and, therefore, of the creation of meaning in the world. It is only on this basis, it seems to me, that we can grasp the real meaning of his famous precept that 'an attitude of moral indifference has no connection with scientific objectivity.'[45]

The suppression of value in sociology

As he attacked the social sciences of his time for their concealment of value,[46] so he would surely have been as horrified at the same tendencies in sociology today. The discipline has boomed, not merely as a subject for study, but as the source of answers to social and economic problems. Sociologists are involved in all kinds of planning, in education, in industrial management and in a host of other public activities which essentially involve the choice, not merely between alternative techniques, but above all between alternative values:[47]

> Meanwhile, however, the social sciences have been clamouring for, and getting power. Social scientists are rapidly moving into an action role and are being used, particularly in industry, as advisors, problem solvers and 'change agents'.

This is not necessarily to say that they should not be thus involved, but that they rarely disclose or regard as problematic the values they serve. They reduce intense conflicts between opposing sets of values to 'problems of communication'. With an unedifying pretence of objectivity, they often explain away movements which stand for values opposed to theirs in terms of the psychological inadequacies, the deficient socialization or the infinite manipulability of their participants. For value, they substitute cost-effectiveness, critical-path analysis, input-output models. And the results, unlike the social scientists implicated in them, are there for all to see—the motorway a few feet from bedroom windows; the new slum, built to accommodate a sentimental sociologist's nostalgia for a community he would never dream of living in himself; and, at the extreme limit of idiocy, the attempt to apply cost-benefit analysis to a Norman church by measuring its value in terms of its insurance.[48] There are times when one is sorely tempted to recall Weber's remark about his fellow-members of the Association for Social Policy: 'It seems to me that today they are in danger of giving just such applause to mechanisation in the sphere of government and politics. For what else have we heard from them?'[49]

It is instructive to look at a concrete example of the ways in which social science has entered the realm of policy-making; namely, that provided by the sociology of education in Britain. It is an example which not only illustrates Weber's point very clearly, but is also especially apposite in that it is very much at the centre of the British sociological tradition. Research into education in this country is almost entirely geared to the theme that has been the raison d'être of most British sociology since the work of Booth and Rowntree; that of working-class deprivation. In fact, for sociology in Britain, educational deprivation has become the contemporary equivalent of material deprivation. Hence the vast amount of research on educational inequalities and their causes, the results of which have constituted a major pressure in educational reform and, in particular, in the gradual shift towards comprehensive education. Here, we see very clearly one of the ways in which British sociology has had a major impact on public policy. But we can also see the unfortunate consequences of the manner in which that impact has been made.

The first of these consequences concerns, again, the realm of value. Clearly, to concentrate on deprivation is an ethical decision. Yet that we should do so is taken to be virtually self-evident. In very much the way that Weber had in mind, the right to educational equality becomes almost a natural right and is therefore built into the sociology of education unquestioned. Once there, the value-judgment involved is taken for granted and the notion of educational deprivation is treated as being merely an heuristic tool. Its ethical nature is thus concealed, and one result of this is that it is not defended in the only terms in which it can be defended—the terms of value—because it is not thought out in those terms. It assumes, to recall Weber's point, that 'conventional self-evidentness' which leaves those who believe in it, and the sociology which propagates it, wide open to the familiar attack on the discipline as a whole for its role in what is now being pejoratively labelled as 'the progressive consensus', and for its alleged responsibility for every kind of social unrest and political protest. That attack is mounted, of course, on the basis of an explicit set of values. It cannot be answered by ignoring, if only by default, the issues of value involved. It cannot be answered by research and yet more research. It can only be answered by the conscious defence of an alternative set of values. In the case of British education, for example, it needs to be consciously proclaimed and argued, after all the research has been done, duplicated and disseminated, that the implementation of comprehensive education is fundamentally a *moral* decision.

M.W.A.M.S.—E

Weber also made the point that this kind of confusion of the moral and empirical realms 'only reduces the particular value of each'.[50] This indicates the second consequence of the particular way in which British sociology is implicated in policy-making. The kind of sociology in question, just as it reduces the value of the moral realm, also reduces the explanatory power of its own analyses. Following the same example, it can be shown that the concentration on educational inequalities as manifestations of deprivation has two consequences. Firstly, it leads to an inadequate discharge of the task it has set itself; namely, the explanation of educational inequalities. The point here is that one cannot begin to explain any social institution without first establishing the meanings all the participants attach to it. Thus one cannot begin to explain educational inequalities without establishing the values attached to education by those subject to the inequalities, not to mention the values attached to the deprived by other groups involved in the education process. Actually to examine those meanings might, however, cast doubt on the self-evident character of the value-judgment involved in the notion of educational deprivation and reveal the sociology based on it to be a 'one-sided viewpoint' (after all, it is not impossible to construct a case to the effect that British education, with its examination obstacle-race and its continued emphasis on cramming, is something of which everyone ought to be deprived). Moreover, meanings are not easily quantifiable (if, indeed, they are quantifiable at all) and the fact-grubbing empiricism of British sociology discards anything upon which statistics cannot easily be imposed. So, whilst we have some impressionistic evidence about participant views of education, our 'hard' research concentrates on those allegedly objective factors, such as the lack of study facilities at home or the number of books on view in the living-room, which miss the important and basic elements in any sociological explanation.

Secondly, the policy-oriented emphasis on measurable deprivation also impoverishes explanation in other spheres of the sociology of education. Once deprivation becomes the central concept and heuristic tool of that specialism, we have no alternative but to fall back, when attempting to account for aspects of education not related to inequalities, upon the only alternative available; namely, the crude framework which 'explains' education in terms of the functions of socialization and training (and which is itself based on an illegitimate translation of an ethical imperative—the problem of order—into a purely logical proposition).[51] Again, the result is an inadequate sociology, a fact demonstrated by its total inability to explain the upheavals and conflicts in higher education in recent years. Certainly, the upsurge of student militancy could never have been predicted on the basis of a conception of education as an agency of socialization. Small wonder, then, that the papers on the sociology of education presented to the 1970 Annual Conference of the British Sociological Association reveal, over and above their intrinsic qualities, a lack of any unifying sociological framework and a sudden, somewhat bewildered search for new frameworks. They demonstrate, in short, the breakdown of both the 'deprivation' and the functionalist versions of the sociology of education in the face of major events in education neither of them can begin to explain.

In the annual report of the Social Science Research Council for 1969-70, it was suggested that, 'perhaps the social sciences would advance faster if the researchers became more integrally related to the work of those responsible for the formulation of public policy'.[52] In fact, it is precisely this kind of relationship that has led so far to inadequate sociology and, to the extent that the findings of sociological research have been influential in policy-making, to inadequately formulated policies. Above all, it has led to the suppression of value in both sociology and public debate over social policy. Unhappily, if not surprisingly, given the promptings of the SSRC and the increasingly overt pressure for a more vocational emphasis in the teaching of sociology in British higher education, it is almost inevitable that this view of the purpose and role of the discipline will become more and more dominant. Again, it is not a question of whether or not we should be involved; simply by doing sociology, as I have tried to show, we are inescapably involved in political and moral commitments. Rather, it is a question of the nature of our involvement and of the need to make it explicit and to build our sociology upon it. As things stand, we also have elevated social science into the arbiter of our moral decisions. We, too, have allowed social science to usurp the moral realm, to the detriment of both.

Ethical neutrality as an ethical imperative

Undoubtedly, Weber would have opposed this as fiercely as he did in his own time and place. But it would not have surprised

him. For he saw it as part of a wider process that was rapidly
becoming almost irresistible:[53]

> The fate of our times is characterised by rationalisation
> and intellectualisation and, above all, by the 'disenchantment
> of the world'. Precisely the ultimate and most sublime
> values have retreated from public life either into the
> transcendental realm of mystic life or into the brotherliness
> of direct and personal human relations.

Science is an expression—indeed, the most complete expression—
of this process. And its invasion of the moral realm represents the
ultimate triumph of rationalization. Yet still Weber could not
accept this triumph. Still he hoped that we might somehow
restore value and recover human creativity in a world so alien to
both:[54]

> The fruit of the tree of knowledge, which is distasteful to
> the complacent, but which is nonetheless inescapable,
> consists in the insight that every single important activity
> and ultimately life as a whole, if it is not to be permitted to
> run on as an event in nature but is instead to be
> consciously guided, is a series of ultimate decisions through
> which the soul . . . chooses its own fate, i.e., the meaning of
> its activity and existence.

In the end, then, the doctrine of ethical neutrality itself has the
character of an ethical imperative. Together with his charismatic
leader, it is Weber's answer to rationalization, to the 'supreme
mastery of the bureaucratic way of life', to his 'great question'—
the problem of control. If this is also becoming our great question,
then the real substance of the doctrine of ethical neutrality for us
is an injunction to social science not to retreat from value, but to
confront it, to reveal and proclaim it as value, and thereby to
preserve the possibility of moral consciousness, moral choice and
moral action.

This, I suggest, is the lesson that Weber's value theory holds
for us, in the situation of sociology and sociologists today. It is
not, as I have said, the lesson drawn from his work on value in the
past. But, as he himself pointed out, every generation draws lessons
from earlier generations that accord with its own preoccupations:[55]

The cultural problems which move men form themselves ever anew and in different colours, and the boundaries of that area in the infinite stream of concrete events which acquires meaning and significance for us . . . are constantly subject to change. The intellectual contexts from which it is viewed and scientifically analysed shift. The points of departure of the cultural sciences remain changeable throughout the limitless future as long as a Chinese ossification of intellectual life does not render mankind incapable of setting new questions to the eternally inexhaustible flow of life.

In a moment of rupture, we set new questions, seek new meanings and points of departure. Inevitably, then, our view of Weber's work will be different from that which has prevailed hitherto. This does not absolve us from justifying our 'one-sided viewpoint' by reference to the evidence of his writings. But, to take the Weberian point, it does make clear the interpretative, value-relevant nature of that viewpoint.

Perhaps the real measure of the richness and significance of any body of work is that it retains the possibility of life through its susceptibility to interpretation and reinterpretation in the light of the concerns of successive generations. By that standard, Weber's work is still urgent and alive. Beyond this, however, its continuing vitality depends upon its unsurpassed statement of the sociological task. For Weber showed, contrary to everything that has since been said about his value theory, precisely how and why sociology *is* geared to that ultimate question:[56] 'what shall we do, and how shall we arrange our lives?'

Notes:

1 Quoted in P. Honigsheim, *On Max Weber*, New York, 1968, p. 14.
2 Here and elsewhere in this chapter, I am indebted to Stuart Hall, Acting Director of the Centre for Contemporary Cultural Studies at the University of Birmingham, whose suggestions in discussion and in Centre seminar papers have been invaluable.
3 The terminology here is borrowed from L. Althusser, *For Marx*, 1969; though I doubt whether the argument it is here used to advance has much in common with the argument of that book.
4 E. Durkheim, *Suicide*, London, 1952; J. D. Douglas, *The Social Meanings of Suicide*, Princeton, 1967.

5   J. Halloran, P. Elliott and G. Murdock, *Demonstrations and Communication: A Case Study*, 1970.

6   S. Cotgrove, *The Science of Society*, 1967, p. 25. I hasten to add that Cotgrove was not discussing Weber when he advanced this proposition. But it happens to be a very clear expression of the view of the fact/value distinction conventionally attributed to Weber, and can thus stand as representative of that attribution.

7   Cf. J. A. Rex's chapter in this volume.

8   Weber, *The Methodology of the Social Sciences*, New York, 1949, p. 25.

9   *Ibid.*, Weber, *Methodology*, p. 63.

10   *Ibid.*. p. 81.

11   *Ibid.*, p. 76.

12   *Ibid.*, pp. 81–2.

13   *Ibid.*, p. 84.

14   *Ibid.*, p. 72.

15   *Ibid.*, p. 57.

16   Quoted in H. Stuart Hughes, *Consciousness and Society*, New York, 1958, p. 290.

17   See J. A. Rex, op. cit.

18   Weber, *Economy and Society*, ed. by G. Roth and C. Wittich, New York, 1968, p. 4.

19   *Ibid.*, p. 14.

20   See A. V. Cicourel, *Methods and Measurement in Sociology*, New York, 1964.

21   See A. Dawe, 'The two sociologies,' *Brit. J. Sociol.*, XXI, 2, June 1970.

22   R. Aron, *Main Currents in Sociological Thought*, vol. 2, 1968, p. v.

23   As opposed to the picture, drawn by the sociology of social system, of interaction as the *derivative* of the social system. For a fuller presentation of the thesis summarized in this paragraph, see Dawe, 'The two sociologies'.

24   Quoted in J. P. Mayer, *Max Weber and German Politics*, 1956, pp. 127–8.

25   Weber, *The Protestant Ethic and the Spirit of Capitalism*, 1930, p. 182.

26   Quoted by H. Gerth and C. Wright Mills (eds), in *From Max Weber*, 1948, p. 55.

27   There is, obviously, a contradiction here, but it should not be assumed that this is a contradiction between the sociology and its ethical base. In fact, it is a contradiction which is outside the scope of this chapter: namely, a contradiction between two opposed ethical concerns and thus between two consequent and opposed sociological orientations in Weber's work. He is undoubtedly concerned with the problem of control, but—as, for example, his defence of the notion of the *Machtstaat* indicates— he is torn between that and a concern with the problem of order. And the latter concern leads to the appearance in his work of

elements of a sociology of social system, which conflict with his definition of sociology in terms of social action.

28 Quoted in P. Jacobs and S. Landau, *The New Radicals*, 1967, p. 69.
29 Weber, *Methodology*, pp. 143–4.
30 *Ibid.*, p. 145.
31 The reference is, of course, to Weber, *The Protestant Ethic*.
32 For this point and further discussion of its significance, see A. Shuttleworth, *Two Working Papers in Cultural Studies*, Occasional Paper No. 2 of the Centre for Contemporary Cultural Studies, University of Birmingham.
33 See, for example, A. V. Cicourel, *The Social Organisation of Juvenile Justice*, New York, 1968.
34 Weber, *Protestant Ethic*, pp. 125–6.
35 *Ibid.*, pp. 181–2.
36 Gerth and Mills, op. cit., p. 246.
37 Weber, 'Science as a vocation' in Gerth and Mills, op.cit., p. 135.
38 Quoted in C. Antoni, *From History to Sociology*, 1962, p. 143.
39 Weber, *Methodology*, p. 57.
40 *Ibid., Methodology*, p. 19.
41 Though it is worth noting just what emerges from such statements about the *content* of Weber's own ethical position. His ethic amounts to a fierce concern for the sanctity of individual moral choice, in his eyes the only possible basis for morality. For him, the moral realm is a world of 'warring gods'. In his words, 'fate, and certainly not science, holds sway over these gods and their struggles' and only the individual can decide 'which is God for him and which is the devil' ('Science as a vocation', p. 148). But if all gods are equal, then there can be no criteria for choosing between them. Morality then becomes a matter of feeling, and what matters is the intensity of moral choice, the consciousness and dedication with which it is made, rather than the nature of the choice itself. In terms of its content, therefore, Weber's ethical position is individualistic to the extent that he becomes ethically neutral in an *ethical* sense. Undoubtedly, this is a dubious moral position. But, in the present context, the point is that even his doctrine of ethical neutrality is a derivative of his conception of the *moral* world. Once again, the sociological prescription is founded on the ethic.
42 Weber, *Methodology*, p. 56.
43 *Ibid.*, p. 38.
44 *Ibid.*, p. 13.
45 *Ibid.*, p. 60.
46 The reference here, of course, is to the prolonged dispute over the role of value judgments in social science, which dominated the proceedings of the Verein für Sozialpolitik (Association for Social Policy) in Germany from 1905 to 1914, and in which Weber was one of the leading and most passionate protagonists.
47 L. Klein (Social Sciences Adviser, Esso Petroleum Co. Ltd), 'Social

science as a threat to society', British Association paper (Section N), Annual Meeting, September 1969.

48   This particular idiocy was perpetrated on behalf of the Roskill Commission on London's third airport. It is worth adding that the role of social research in the Commission's inquiries constitutes one of the most dramatic and monstrous demonstrations in recent years of the dangers of research of this value-suppressive, quantifi-maniac kind. Indeed, the role of social scientists in the work of the Roskill Commission deserves an inquiry of its own. Meanwhile, see Peter Self's brief, but excellent discussion of the issues at stake in 'Nonsense on stilts: the futility of Roskill', *New Society*, 2 July 1970.

49   Quoted in Mayer, op. cit., p. 126.

50   Weber, *Methodology*, p. 12.

51   See Dawe, op. cit.

52   Quoted in *New Society*, 13 August 1970, p. 291.

53   Weber, 'Science as a vocation', p. 155.

54   Weber, *Methodology*, p. 18.

55   *Ibid.*, p. 84.

56   Quoted from Tolstoi by Weber in 'Science as a vocation', p. 152.

Four

Arun Sahay

The importance of Weber's methodology in sociological explanation

Weber's methodology—let me, at the risk of being banal, point out—is not a system of techniques of survey and data analysis. It deals with the fundamental problems of scientific knowledge: its nature, limits and possibilities. Furthermore, Weber's is the only methodology in the whole of sociological thought which has *explicitly* solved the practical—as opposed to the metaphysical and emotional—problems of sociological analysis. It seems to make incursions into metaphysics, philosophy and aesthetics, which can be disturbing only if science is felt to be something tangibly factual. Incidentally, it is through Weber's discussion of the methodological principles of social sciences that one realizes the completeness and importance of Pareto's theory and methodology, and is able to judge *others'* theories on their merits.[1]

Weber's interest in sociology was many-sided, converging, as such an interest must do, on the definition of the subject itself. According to Alexander von Schelting's interpretation of Weber's methodology[2]—which is the only independent and definitive analysis available, in German, English or French, of Weber's methodological ideas in the context of the logical problem of social-scientific knowledge—the theme of Weber's sociology was the process of rationalization of life, both in its historical development, that is, in modern times, and in its inherent logical problem of translation from subjective rationality to objective knowledge. In this theme we can detect the immediacy as well as the core of sociology. Sociology is necessarily a modern science. It cannot be traditional or given. For traditionality or givenness is consistent with a way of life in which the modes of change and innovation are bound by an unchanging mode of thought. Modernity, on the other hand, is the result of those ways of life in which neither the modes of change nor the modes of thought are accepted without question; in which there are, in other words, no axiomatic feelings of any substance. The premise of modernity is that historical or social change occurs through man's varying and conflicting evaluations of his existence. Sociology, thus, becomes possible. There are some who have argued—and still argue in spite of Weber—that existence, then, is the source of one's understanding. But to understand existence is not to create it : existence is given.

This *seemingly* paradoxical notion of understanding is the first principle of Weber's theory of sociological knowledge. Understanding, for Weber, is not the subtle intuitive sympathy which philosophers favour—but intellectual, analytical and predictive explanation of action. It is a clear scientific delimitation of *verstehen*, that German word which is used in many textbooks and commentaries to designate Weber as an intuitionist, idealist-rationalist, pessimist or, even, an apologist for the capitalist ideology.

Action is the basis of any analysis in Weber's view. It is not a new term for behaviour, as it is in Talcott Parsons's sociology, but a specific, clear and irrefutable primary concept of sociological analysis. If one analyses the concept of behaviour in comparison with action, one finds that behaviour is what one observes and motive is what one infers—if it is not already aprioristically assumed : and action *is the motive and behaviour together*, in a means-end relationship, for any behaviour is meaningless without its motive, and a motive cannot be determined without any behaviour. This relationship between the observed and the inferred data—which has given rise to a tedious and speculative literature—can be understood simply, if one realizes that when one is dealing with *social* action, it has to be established between social motive and behaviour; and, when one is dealing with action as itself, between psychological motive—which includes internalized social motives—and individual behaviour and so on. It cannot be understood if one presents it as an a priori assumption, as the well-known clichés of sociology—i.e. instincts, needs, class interests, consensus and ideological conflicts etc.—are presented.

To understand social action, therefore, Weber faced the problem of making both immediate action and historical action explicable within the same analytic framework. This framework has confused many contemporary sociologists, because immediate action, which has a living, psychological source, becomes independent of it as historical action. Thus, psychology and history seem to them unrelated, and consequently, they offer three independent definitions of sociology.

The first kind is offered by those for whom history is a series of dates and names, and psychology is the ultimate source of sociological explanation. For them, sociology is intuitive, sympathetic understanding of other people's behaviour and motives, to be presented in the form of typical action. Secondly, for those who do not hold with psychology, sociology is simply a step beyond historical narration and embodies the results of what they call the 'comparative' approach. Thirdly, there are those still who follow the traditional division of discipline by subject-matter. They hold that sociology is neither psychologically nor historically oriented. For them, behaviour is a fact, and, 'everyone knows, facts speak for themselves': and theory, analysis, objectivity and values are all codifiable items, and measurement per se is the ultimate objectivity.

It is the analytic framework, i.e. the *logical relationship* between theory and analysis, objectivity and values, description and explanation—which all these three kinds of sociologists assert as their given premise—that exposes their inadequacy and vagueness when compared to Weber. His methodology is precisely about this relationship, and it is not difficult to see how important this question is for any science, let alone sociology. Sociology, in fact, has always had the problems which have become important for natural sciences only recently : as they have progressed, in practice, from observation and experiment through inferential generalization to a priori theoretical explanation of microcosmic phenomena.

In sociology, the process of explanation cannot be linear and cumulative : it has to be simultaneous. For example, as I mentioned earlier, observation and classification of behaviour for its own sake, or without reference to its relationship to motive, psychological or social (in the widest sense of the terms), is meaningless. In the usual kind of sociology the causal imputation in correlations is always given, because the hypothesis starts with a determinist assumption. But for Weber causal imputation is *to determine* which of the equally, or independently, variable correlates is *in fact* causally significant. In other words, Weber's methodology allows one to decide, in specific contexts, whether action is caused by the value or the value itself has arisen as a result of action. Therefore, those who expect sociological explanations to be in the form of determinist assertions are unable to judge the significance of Weber's Protestant ethic thesis, and the related studies in the sociology of religion, which, altogether, form the only complete application by Weber of his methodology.

This new perspective on sociological analysis is the direct result of his fundamental concept of value-relevance. If Weber's methodology is to be of any use, the concept of value-relevance can only mean what Weber himself meant by it. He took the formulation of value-relevance from Heinrich Rickert's refutation of the notion of effectiveness—or, simply, that whatever happens is history—as a principle of selection of facts in history, presented by the historian Eduard Meyer. Both Rickert and Weber were agreed on the form of value-relevance, and the refutation of effectiveness, up to the point that the mere occurrence of events does not make them historical, but the historical is that which has a value or a meaning.

Rickert's solution to the question, 'which values or meanings the historian should refer to?' was that as there are suprahistorical values which all civilized men accept, they should, therefore, be the basis of selecting historical facts. Weber rejected this solution, because it begged the question, 'who are civilized?' The historian could only refer to his own notions of civilized values, and inevitably evaluate all history from his own subjective position. Then, the whole basis of value-relevance, the individuality and uniqueness of actual meanings and significance which men cherish and live by would be destroyed. Weber's solution was brilliantly simple: he made value-relevance the principle which governs the description of facts by clarifying first the value inherent in the context, or the situation, under analysis—whether one is concerned with one's own action or someone else's behaviour or with a momentous event in history or the social relevance of an intrinsically meaningless course of natural process. It is this simple definition of value-relevance by Weber which cuts through the whole problem of understanding, which seems completely insoluble if one takes all the objects of understanding—historical processes social-psychological motives, metaphysical and aesthetic ideas, sentiments, above all, the rationality of knowledge itself—and their complex characteristics into account.

The basic difficulty which the philosophical problem of understanding presents is the reconciliation of the meaninglessness of natural reality and the value or meaning of social reality. Rickert and Dilthey, whose philosophical solutions are directly relevant here, as they form the philosophical background of Weber's methodology, suggested in their respective formulations that meaning is either an accretion to the object of understanding or is inextricable from it. A. von Schelting rightly points out in his critique that Weber did not offer any *philosophical* solution of his own to this alternative. He simply took what was practicable in both Rickert's[3] and Dilthey's[4] formulations, and, in fact, gave a perfectly operative solution for sociology. (Between Dilthey and Rickert the intervening figure is that of W. Windelband. In his Rectoral address to the University of Strassburg in 1894— 'Geschichte und Naturwissenschaft', reprinted in *Präludien*, Tübingen, 1919—Windelband gave a distinction between history and natural science which clarifies the whole basis of the debate between individualizing and generalizing methods in sociology. Rickert, stimulated by Weber's ideas, refined the whole conception by treating individualizing and generalizing methods as 'polar extremes' of scientific work (see his preface to the sixth and seventh German edition of *Science and History*). Weber's contribution to the whole debate is an outstanding and definitive reconciliation between the two extremes, which Rickert could not achieve, in the historical-social sciences. The point—which could have resolved the puzzled and confused feelings of many commentators on what Weber *did* accomplish—is that the major influence on the division of labour involved in the works of Rickert, Weber and Troeltsch, between the philosophical discussion of value-relevant description, the ideal-typical analysis of ethic and action as a sociological theory and the systematic study of the social teaching of the Christian churches as an application of Weber's theory, is that of Weber.) Understanding in sociology, according to Weber— as pointed out earlier—is intellectual understanding of social reality in terms of action : therefore the meaning of an action is a given datum of analysis—whether it appears as an accretion or as a part of the object. The sociologist can only analyse the interpretations which people give of their own or others' actions : he cannot grasp, hold or fix the actual process of any action, immediate or historical, simply because it is mental. In a sociological interpretation the meaning of an action is all that can be determined and, Weber would add, whether this meaning is rational, value-oriented, traditional or emotional. Therefore, to reconcile the different arguments of philosophers is hardly relevant to sociology.

Although philosophical arguments can—and in fact do—make the characteristics of a concept explicit, they cannot be used to justify the concept as a valid means of analysis. The concept of ideal type in Weber's methodology is an example which makes this point quite clearly. Weber used the characteristics of the concept of understanding, which both Rickert and Dilthey made explicit through their different philosophical analyses, to formulate the ideal type and one can recognize four different characterizations of it. The task which Weber faced was to make the four characterizations, based on the philosophical arguments on understanding, both consistent with each other and applicable to sociological explanation. This is a point which, because present-day philosophers of social science and sociologists are unable to differentiate between philosophical concepts or characterizations and their empirical applicability, has been completely lost sight of in contemporary sociological and philosophical writings. If one has considered the four forms of ideal types, which von Schelting, among the many commentators on Weber, is the only one to recognize in their consistent relationship, the whole debate about generalizing and individualizing method, and between behaviourism and phenomenology, seems like obtuse puppetry.

These are, if we take the individualizing forms first: (1) the ideal type which makes the characteristics of a unique action or event explicit and, (2) the ideal type which makes the ideas of an action clear and consistent.

Then, the generalizing forms of the ideal type, which are similarly distinct: (1) the ideal type which organizes correlated facts to allow imputation of a causal relationship between them; (2) the ideal type which conceptualizes the basic, general characteristics of a social action in its pure form.

Let me at this point give a simple positive definition of the ideal type as a whole—as much has been made of Weber's negative definition—for we are now in a position to see the basis of Weber's sociological analysis. *An ideal type is a logically consistent description, from a specific, or given, point of view which makes the means-end relationship of the action, event, process or interpretation of ideas, unambiguous, to enable one to translate* disparate, fragmentary ideas, interpretations or correlations into scientifically explicable terms. The ideal-type concept, in fact, is the realization of the principle of sociological rationality, which is Weber's basic and original contribution to scientific analysis. Its contents are only relatively objective, and the purpose of sociological analysis is to decide which particular one—or a combination—of these relatively objective but *possible* descriptions of facts is the completely valid one, i.e., which gives the correct cause of an event or action.

These ideal types have been invariably seen by sociologists as irreconcilably generalizing and individualizing. This view has given rise to a whole range of theories, typologies as well as critiques. In fact, it has become such a fashionable word that any arbitrary description which one cannot justify, either on the basis of evidence or theoretical analysis, is blithely called ideal-typical. What has been ignored, or not seen at all, by the contemporary sociologists is that the formal basis of all the four kinds of substantive ideal types is exactly the same. They are all concerned with the logical relationship between the value, which may have determined the ideas, actions and events to be analysed, and the *results* of the ideas, actions and events. Weber's basic point is that sociological analysis is in terms of values, individuality and understanding, and the four forms of ideal type are the various means of relating these methodological principles, each depending on the particular kind of material.

One may ask at this point how can these principles be related in exactly the same way, whatever the material? Weber's procedure is, first, to clarify the value inherent in the process of action, i.e., the significance or the meaning of the action to be analysed. This significance can either be personal, psychological, social or historical, which will be revealed by the *interpretation* of the action which is given by the actor or the participant. It is noticeable that in fact no concrete action is analysed in sociology, but its interpretation—a point which makes Weber's view of sociological analysis very similar to Pareto's, and quite unlike the present day 'action' theorists. Since interpretations are the raw data of sociology—not a reification of interpretation as the action itself, as in all forms of behaviourism—the whole point about value-relevance, meaning and understanding becomes immediately *unambiguous*. This also shows how the three descriptive sources of sociological analysis, history, sociography and social anthropology, can in fact be translated into sociology.

The second step in Weber's sociological explanation is the construction of the ideal-typical norm of comparison, with which the given interpretation is compared, to enable one to impute a cause to the correlated facts of the interpretation, either internally or externally.

The third step of the ideal-typical analysis is generalization from such individual causal imputations.

The final step is, quite logically, abstraction, which enables one to make conditional predictions of social change. This is because, for Weber, sociology is nothing but the understanding of the processes of social change. Definitions, concepts, categories, typologies are for him only instruments of this understanding. They are not valid in themselves, because they have to be formulated a priori. It is this last point which makes Weber quite different from the 'theoretical' sociologists of today, who have not been able to distinguish as clearly as Weber *between* the practical coincidence of definitions, concepts, categories and typologies with abstractions of empirical analysis *and* their logical separateness.

Moreover, they, for whom the pure types, for example, of authority or bureaucracy, constitute Weber's sociological theory, and the studies in economy and society his sociological analysis, would do well to understand the basic analytical framework—which is Weber's most enduring contribution to sociology—and realize that it can be superseded neither by reformulating the definitional concepts nor by introducing substantive amendments to his *inferences* on the nature of the Protestant ethic, the forms of capitalism or the industrial society or the so-called aristocracy of Prussian Junkers etc.; neither by asserting that his study of China is not really historical and that he was quite right about India, nor that Ancient Judaism contained the seeds of modernity' and therefore Judaism should be the real source of modern industrial bourgeois society. Such amendments and improvements are legitimate refutations of his methodology only if they show that it is impossible to apply the methodology, as it is given, *and arrive at* conclusions and definitions which are *consistent* with Weber's. Otherwise, they remain projections of subjective judgments, depending for their importance, or lack of it, *only* on the critic's limitations in taste, experience, knowledge and, above all, discernment.

Neither of the two kinds of contemporary improvers on Weber is able to see the inevitable relationship between a priori theorizing and empirical reference. A priori theorizing for Weber was governed by the correctness of methodological principles, and empirical reference inevitably meant causal imputation. Causal imputation, as Weber formulated it, is not a correlation between a metaphysical deterministic principle—like evolution, historical dialectics, functional equilibrium or the need for meaning and sense—and actual behaviour, but a discovery of the relationship between the factors one infers from, and the observed situations which seem to associate in, *empirical* reality—which is, in effect, a logical use of theory and empirical research.

This may not seem a plain statement in relation to the more recent theorists, whose claim to importance rests almost entirely on their assertion of having gone beyond Weber, as one finds certain mysteries in their judgment and understanding of the nature of sociological explanation.

The person who has influenced most, in the last forty years or so, such developments in sociology is Karl Mannheim.[5] An analytic comparison of Weber's methodology and his sociology of knowledge was made by Alexander von Schelting in his book on methodology, which could be considered a forewarning of the development of sociology in its preoccupation with subjective involvement and in its metaphysical notions of systematic knowledge. But what it more interesting is the influence his theoretical ideas have had on the axiomatic feelings of the present generation of sociologists, especially of those who explicitly acknowledge their debt to Weber rather than to Mannheim.

Of these the most basic is that of systematization, which Mannheim introduced in his doctoral dissertation published in 1922, called *The Structural Analysis of Epistemology*. The notion of systematization is basically a description of the process of reasoning. It might not have done any harm if Mannheim had left it in this form: but he garnished it with the idea that every concept is a link in the unending chain of ideas. To this garnish he added the spice of three independently valid contexts of truth: ontological, psychological and logical. Of these he admitted that the logical was the most sound, but nevertheless, since there are always several theories floating about and accepted by people as true, they all must somehow be true. So truth is, Mannheim concluded, what is existentially possible. One thing in Mannheim leads to another: the criterion of judging knowledge is, therefore, the value-position of an individual with his specific location in time and space. His sociology of knowledge is thus the empirical realization of all these metaphysical and epistemological ideas and interpretations—with an element which is at once pleasing, practical and human, and which has been the most effective source of his popularity: i.e. *the* custodians of true and rational knowledge are the intelligentsia, who are free from the fetters of their class ideology and the false but possible social theories.

What are the axiomatic feelings which Mannheim created for today's sociologists? (1) That a priori theoretical statements are true simply by having been made by a subject on an object. (2) Every social datum is part of a theorized structure. (3) The sociologist cannot be *intellectually* detached from the materials of his research. (4) But nevertheless, he has committed himself to objectivity. It is a commandment which he must strive to obey, even if he can never succeed. (5) We must intervene in the rational reorganization of society as *sociologists*—because what we say is true *because* we say so—since rationality is the norm of action in sociology.

The most well-known development of these axiomatic feelings is in the works of Talcott Parsons.[6] He has—more than anybody else—taken sociology far in its a priori *systematics*, metaphysically functional relation of theory and research and in its mixture of involvement in the moral problem of order and rationality and commitment to objectivity. For him—as for Mannheim—rationality is the perfect norm, which objectifies even the most subjective and arbitrary idea. One need only read two of his early articles to see the blueprint of his theoretical structure—which he has been building and refining for the last thirty-five years. These articles are 'The place of ultimate values in sociological theory', published in *Ethics*, 1935, and 'The role of theory in social research', published in *American Sociological Review*, 1938.

Parsons interprets the Weberian means-end relationship as an analytical framework in the same way as Mannheim interprets the process of rational thought as systematization. Ultimate values, as a system, become simply an accretion to the behaviourist framework. His several categories of 'means' and 'ends' are nothing but abstract *descriptions* of what appears to him, in substance, to be a continuum from mere behaviour to rational action. This end-category of rational action is not what Weber meant by the specific, substantive means-end relationship of action, which determined the kind of rationality (which has, intrinsically, the same structure in all cases) an action could be said to have—like end-rationality, value-rationality, traditional rationality or affectual (emotional) rationality, but what Mannheim meant by his definition of both substantial and functional rationality. Mannheim distinguished two kinds of rationality which in Weber's categories would be included in end-rationality and value-rationality, but Parsons quite rightly would have only one kind of rationality. Yet, rationality is not defined by the logical inevitability of the means-end relationship, or by the structure of action, but by the action being willed, or not. Therefore, in actual fact, Weber's four ways of distinguishing any real rational action, are changed by Mannheim to two categories of rationality itself, on the basis of the contents of action, and by Parsons to one category of rationality on the basis of whether the action was voluntary (or, simply, willed) or not. All action by very definition is willed; therefore its rationality or irrationality cannot depend on the will but on its internal relationship between its end, means and conditions or, simply, its structure. So what is in Weber a perfect tool of sociological analysis, indeed, a definition of rationality in its sociological context, gets lost in a single notion of a dubious amalgam of definitions and hypotheses as ultimate explanations. In this example, we find a perfect expression of the first axiomatic feeling—that a theory is what an individual *thinks* the actual relationships are or should be—and that what he deduces from his thought, or arbitrary assumption, is the same as what he can empirically determine and generalize upon. In other words, if one succeeds in producing a set of deductive propositions from one's subjective notions on life and social relations, it is valid by itself. Because if it is possible, then it is true. So sociological theory is produced by everyone who can produce a set of self-validating propositions. This has become a truism only because of Karl Mannheim. For him, sociology is not an art because it does not contain an internally valid assumption of truth. It is also not a science because it does not have a single transcendent criterion of truth. It is *a branch of philosophy* which has both an internally valid criterion of truth and an object to refer to: the eternal problems of existence. Therefore it has a threefold criterion—which, in fact, contains three independent criteria—of truth (existence as an individual finds it) and the three aspects of individual consciousness, which he would designate as existential, psychological and logical, governing, as a troika, the truth of his sociology.

Not enough tribute has been paid to Mannheim, who was *the* inventor of contemporary sociology.

This self-congratulating logic has had a dramatic effect in the interpretation of Weber's fundamental methodological principle, that of value-relevance. It has been interpreted, without any clear acknowledgement, but faithfully, according to Mannheim's subjective vision of a 'rationally' planned world, which the Intellectual would preside over as the Creator. Although Parsons' description of it as the scientist's interest may seem to be a reasonable compromise between Mannheim and Weber: but, on analysis, one finds that although the scientist's interest in a problem or a subject of research will be individual, indeed arbitrary: yet he is inevitably objective by virtue of his culture and education and role in society; a definition remarkably similar to Mannheim's.

This interpretation of value-relevance is the prevailing dogma of sociologists in the United States and their associates in the rest of the world, even of those who are designated as the Conflict School and considered to be of a directly opposed view. In cases of theories being opposed in this substantive way, the simple question, which arises when such a total refutation is made, is: if societies are not based on consensus as the universal determinant, then how can they be based on any other such substantive-descriptive notion? The simple answer to this question—which has not so far been answered by contemporary sociologists, but which was answered by Weber—is that we must look for the causes which have determined individual events, specific situations as well as the causes which determine the generalized forms of various *kinds* of action which we find in the history of the world: and finally, what can one predict—on the basis of the past—for the future? This answer is possible, as it should be clear by now, only on the principles which are formulated and interrelated in Weber's methodology; and not by speculating on the basis of society's existence.

It may perhaps be appropriate to end with such an intuitionist interpretation of Weber's methodology, which seems to have become the recent favourite among an increasing number of contemporary sociologists: Alfred Schutz's[7] theory of social action: so that one could judge conclusively whether Weber's methodology does need any modification or not. In his article, 'The Social World and the Theory of Social Action', first published in *Social Research* in 1960, Alfred Schutz presents a simplified, personalized version of what has become known as the subjective point of view. His definition of social action is the same as Weber's, but his interpretation of action—that is, its understanding—is as rigid in its fixed and imposed relationship between concept and reality as that of any behaviourist. While the behaviourist seems to ignore the subjective aspect of action, i.e., the motive or justification of behaviour, the phenomenologist gives the motives and justifications—which Schutz calls the 'because' and 'in-order-to' motives— a prominent place in his assertions. Both take a stereotype of motives and justifications of the given situation as the norm of behaviour or action, and 'explain' or 'understand' it. The subjectivity of the behaving 'unit', i.e., participant or actor or whatever an individual is called—is necessarily neglected in both the behaviourist's as well as the phenomenologist's scheme of things. For both, the scientist is a role player, and in both, surprisingly, he remains detached as an observer. The difference between their points of view lies only in that the behavioural scientist judges his behaving unit from his hypothesis, and the phenomenologist steps out of his role of scientist for a moment to play 'Caesar or a cave-man'—to borrow Schutz's example—to understand his phenomenon's 'typical' motives. In both cases therefore, the source of judgment, the norm of behaviour, lies *in the subjectivity of the scientist himself*—and not in the behaviour or the motivated act or even their actual context.

Although Schutz appears to interpret Weber more faithfully than others, his method of ideal-typical construction—or rather 'reconstruction', to use his own word—of reality, betrays his complete misunderstanding of Weber's ideal types as a means of sociological explanation; indeed, of all his methodological principles, if one compared them. If Schutz had, of course, developed an independent methodology on the basis of phenomenological assumptions, the comparison could not be so direct and devastating, as he must suffer when he is explicitly modifying Weber.

In Schutz's scheme, when we find that—and I quote *verbatim*—
'it is the destiny of the personal ideal type to play the role the
actor in the social world would have to adopt to perform the
typical act', we wonder, quite rightly, whether Weber's ideal type
is really as unworkable as such a reinterpretation would indicate.
Schutz goes on to say (p. 220):

> And as the type is constructed in such a way that it
> performs exclusively typical acts, the objective and
> subjective elements in the formation of unit-acts coincide.
> On the other hand, the formation of the type, the choice of
> the typical event, and the elements considered as typical are
> conceptual terms which can be discussed objectively and
> which are open to criticism and verification. They are not
> formed by social scientists at random and without check or
> restraint.

It seems from this passage that social scientists need constant
reassurance that they are not randomly and unrestrainedly subjective, and that their state of anxiety forms a cloud over those
principles and methods and ideas which should demonstrate their
work as objective and scientific if they took the trouble of examining and applying them.

This criticism might seem misplaced if one read Schutz's article
further, and looked at the rules of conduct that he formulates for
sociologists:

(1) on *relevance*: 'the problem, once chosen by the social
scientist, creates a scheme of reverence and . . . limits the scope
within which relevant ideal types might be formed';

(2) on *adequacy*: 'each scientific term must be so constructed
that a human act performed within the life world by an
individual actor in the way indicated by the typical construction
would be reasonable and understandable for the actor himself as
well as his fellow men . . .';

(3) on *logical consistency*: 'the system of ideal types must
remain in full compatibility with the principles of formal
logic . . .';

(4) on *compatibility*: 'the system of ideal types must contain
only scientifically verifiable assumptions, which have to be fully
compatible with the whole of our scientific knowledge . . .' (see
pp. 220–21).

These are echoes of those feelings and sentiments with which the sociologist has been exhorting himself in the name of science and objectivity. The question that he should have asked, but did not, is whether sociology is to remain a cult-worship or a practical, analytical science, which it has been shown by Weber it can be. But it would seem that he prefers the eternal problems of existence as the subject matter of sociology to remain eternal problems: and would make sociology the kind of philosophy which Mannheim imagined it to be—with the support of the 'philosophers of social science' of today—when what he lacks is, it seems to me, the simple ability to analyse and to connect.

Notes:

1   See my editorial comment, 'Some ideas on sociological analysis', in *Sociological Analysis: A Discussion Journal of Research and Ideas*, University of Sheffield, vol. I, no. 1, October 1970, for a fuller discussion of this statement.

2   A. von Schelting, *Max Webers Wissenschaftslehre*, J. C. B. Mohr, Tübingen, 1934.

3   H. Rickert, *Science and History* (trans. by G. Reisman), Van Nostrand, Princeton, 1962.

4   W. Dilthey on 'Understanding', in Patrick Gardiner, *Theories of History*, Free Press, Chicago, 1959.

5   K. Mannheim, *Essays on Sociology and Social Psychology*, Routledge & Kegan Paul, London, 1953; and *Man and Society in an Age of Reconstruction*, Routledge & Kegan Paul, London, 1940.

6   T. Parsons, 'The place of ultimate values in sociological theory', *Ethics*, 1935; and 'The role of theory in social research', *American Sociological Review*, February 1938.

7   A. Schutz, 'The social world and the theory of social action', *Social Research*, Summer 1960.

Five

Robert Moore

History, economics and religion: A review of 'The Max Weber Thesis' thesis

The charge of historical naïveté is often levelled at Weber by British historians. He is accused of adopting a *simpliste* approach to the question of the relations between religion and social change. This charge cannot be substantiated; it seems to be founded on a reading of the essays *The Protestant Ethic and Spirit of Capitalism* only and takes no account of this work's place in Weber's *Religionssoziologie* and his historical and comparative studies. The ignorance of historians is perhaps epitomized in Fischoff's comments on F. H. Knight.[1] Knight translated Weber's *General Economic History* but comments on Weber's sociology of religion in a way which suggests, incredibly, that he was unaware of Weber's comparative studies of world religions.

According to Fischoff, 'The whole historical work of Weber has ultimately one prime object: the understanding of contemporary western culture, especially modern capitalism.'[2] In seeking part of this understanding in the Reformation Weber adopted a course that would have been approved by Marc Bloch, who believed that the Reformation was probably the single most important factor affecting contemporary life in Europe—more important indeed than many subsequent series of events. But in *The Protestant Ethic* Weber affirmed that he had 'no intention whatever of maintaining such a foolish and doctrinaire thesis as that the spirit of capitalism . . . could only have arisen as the result of certain effects of the Reformation'.[3] 'I have again and again been accused of this,' Weber says in a footnote [p. 217]. This particular discussion with its clear disclaimer of any simple causal relation between Protestantism and capitalism cannot be seen apart from Weber's wider sociological concerns. In *The Religion of China* and *The Religion of India* Weber asks the negative question; why did capitalism not develop in these non-European societies? The same question could be asked of the Italian city states which became commercial centres and were regarded by Weber as transitional between the oriental city and the Western capitalist city.[4]

Weber's method in *The Protestant Ethic* is to construct ideal types of capitalist spirit and the Protestant ethic. By ideal type he means 'a complex of elements associated in historical reality which we unite into a conceptual whole from the standpoint of their cultural significance'.[5] The elements chosen are thus selected in accordance with Weber's intellectual definition of the problem, in this case, the religious factors contributing to the economic rationalism of the West. It would not be possible to derive types of economic activity from a logico-deductive treatment of Calvinist theological formulations. To attempt to do so would in itself, however, be to posit a connection which can only be assumed on the basis of a pre-existing historical understanding (which may be only an approximate understanding). One cannot begin with a perfected ideal type; one works from the 'best conceptual formulation . . . that is best from the point of view which interests us here'[6] towards a sharper definition of the concept. This is to be done as a result of using the first approximation as a basis for historical inquiry.

The first approximations are constructed directly from concrete cases, virtually using the actors' own accounts of the situation. The spirit of capitalism is typified by the writings of Benjamin Franklin. For Weber, Franklin represents the 'pure' spirit of capitalism, his work has a 'classical purity' and is free of directly religious influence.[7] The ideal-typical Protestant orientation to the world of social and economic affairs is based mainly on parts of the Westminster Confession and the writings of Richard Baxter. Weber selects and thus accentuates those features of Calvinism which are relevant to the historical problem, those features which 'gave a direction to practical conduct and held the individual to it'.[8]

Understanding the congruence between the capitalist and the Protestant spirit is ultimately a subjective activity. The sociologist puts himself in the place of the traditional Catholic businessman, the Calvinist and the capitalist entrepreneur and views the world in the light of their respective goals and presuppositions. But this is not a matter of instinctive intuition but an activity made possible by extensive historical research and the abstraction of relevant aspects of the subjects' *Weltanschauungen* in accordance with the scholar's intellectual interest. It is necessary, in other words, to develop a comparative approach to the subject; this Weber was doing throughout his work. In developing a comparative approach he developed further typologies of, for example, religious groups, economic enterprise and legitimate authority. He attempted to put the ideal types into the formal sociological structure of his comparative sociology in *Wirtschaft und Gesellschaft* (see Rex, above).

In *The Protestant Ethic* Weber does not directly confront the question of causal analysis. He deals 'only with the affinity between religious precepts and the self-discipline of mundane conduct'.[9] This work is thus 'an exposition of the rich congruency of such diverse aspects of culture as religion and economics. The essay should be considered as a stimulating project in hermeneutics, a demonstration of interesting correlations between diverse cultural factors.'[10] What follows is not an attempt to evaluate the problems that arise from the use of Weber's methods in this field of study. This essay is an attempt to expound Weber on Protestantism and capitalism in the light of such of his sociological work as is now available in English, and in the light of the record of historians.

In his last lectures, published posthumously as *General Economic History*, Weber introduces the Protestant ethic theme in the final chapter. Early parts of the book analyse the development of agrarian property systems and pre-capitalist industry and mining. The origin of modern capitalism includes consideration of trade, colonial policy, technical change, the development of citizenship and the state. Amongst the necessary pre-conditions of modern capitalism he lists the free market for labour and commodities, rational capital accounting, calculable law, formally free labour, rational technology and the commercialization of economic life.[11] In *General Economic History*, Weber cites both cotton manufacture and the steam locomotive as the most important factors in the rise of modern capitalism. There is no 'foolish and doctrinaire thesis' about the role of religion.

On the publication of the Fischoff translation of *The Sociology of Religion* Benjamin Nelson said: 'Nowhere has Weber written so sensitively and learnedly . . . about the interplay of religious and social existence in the Catholic world. Anyone henceforth proposing to write about the problems posed in his *Protestant Ethic* overlooks these pages at his own peril.'[12] 'These pages' are now available in English in *Economy and Society* to be read in their context of Weber's systematic sociology. Especially when read with chapter XVI (originally 'The City' in English) they underline the error of the critics, who are largely answered by the work they seem to have ignored (see below).

Chapter XVI outlines the importance of the city (and Christianity) in creating new social relationships cutting across and replacing class, kinship etc. The unity of the city, the sworn brotherhood, was symbolized by the coming together of all citizens at the Lord's Table. These new relations and the unity of the city facilitated the rise of markets and enterprises that were to be vital in the rise of capitalism (and new social divisions and inequalities): [13]

> The urban population of late medieval Northern Europe had already been well prepared for the doctrines of the Reformation by virtue of institutions which provided a single ethical standard in business and community controls on legal procedure and personal conduct, an oath-bound confederation similar to congregational church government, a destruction of kinship group connections in favour of free association of individuals, and a weakening of traditional sanctions by the separation of the family from commerce and industry.

In the discussion of the rise of capitalism it is not Protestantism only which is regarded as significant amongst religious influences. What then was the significance of Protestantism? Weber suggests that there was 'an affinity between economic rationalism and certain types of rigoristic ethical religion'.[14] Throughout *The Protestant Ethic and the Spirit of Capitalism* Weber advances the notion that Protestantism was an important cause of individual motivation to, and legitimation of, continuous, rational economic enterprise, as a vocation. This does not 'cause' capitalism, it introduces the disciplined, vocational attitude to human activity which is a feature of the capitalist spirit. The argument does, however, go beyond this relatively simple, though methodologically problematic, statement. Protestantism was not only important at the individual motivational level; it also constituted a radical cultural break with tradition and brought into being new kinds of social groups and institutions which were also to be important for the rise and continuation of capitalism.

Individual motivation

The most familiar part of the argument and the substance of *The Protestant Ethic* is succinctly summarized by Weber himself in *Economy and Society* :[15]

> Furthermore, only in the Protestant ethic of vocation does the world, despite all its creaturely imperfections, possess unique and religious significance as the object through which one fulfills his duties by rational behaviour according to the will of an absolutely transcendental god. When success crowns rational, sober, purposive behaviour of the sort not oriented to worldly acquisition, such success is construed as a sign that god's blessing rests upon such behaviour. This innerworldly asceticism had a number of distinctive consequences not found in any other religion. This religion demanded of the believer, not celibacy, as in the monk, but the avoidance of all erotic pleasure, not poverty, but the elimination of all idle and exploitative enjoyment of unearned wealth and income, and the avoidance of all feudalistic, sensuous ostentation of wealth; not the ascetic death-in-life of the cloister, but an alertly, rationally controlled patterning of life, and the avoidance of all surrender to the beauty of the world, to art, or to one's own moods and emotions. The clear and uniform goal of this asceticism was the disciplining and methodical organization of conduct. Its typical representative was the 'man of a vocation' or 'professional' (Berufsmensch), and its unique result was the rational organization of social relationships.

The critics of Weber have concentrated on this aspect of his work. It has been suggested by Trevor-Roper[16] that the notion of 'calling' is Erastian and not peculiarly Calvinist. The point can be conceded with the comment that it is a New Testament idea. Weber's point concerns the special emphasis on 'calling' in Protestant theology linked with the idea of the world in which man fulfills his calling, having religious significance.

Trevor-Roper also shows that the early entrepreneurs were émigrés forced from commercial cities by the Counter-Reformation. They were not pious Calvinists. The examples he cites are what Weber calls 'political capitalists' whose business was supplying governmental credit, meeting the financial needs of the state: 'None of these strata has ever been the primary carrier of an ethical or salvation religion.'[17] Trevor-Roper makes an important point; we should examine the effect on the spread of capitalism of the replacement of merchant elites by elites of office-holders in the mercantilist cities. But this point does not engage with Weber's argument.

Samuelsson's attempted 'definitive rebuttal of Weber's thesis'[18] largely falls on the failure to relate *The Protestant Ethic* to Weber's other works; he 'never discusses Weber's thought in its broad comparative context'.[19] Samuelsson suggests that the acquisitive spirit has always existed; Weber agreed.[20]

> The notion that our rationalistic and capitalistic age is characterised by a stronger economic interest than other periods is childish; the moving spirits of modern capitalism are not possessed of a stronger economic impulse than, for example, an oriental trader. The unchaining of the economic interest merely as such has produced only irrational results; such men as Cortez and Pizarro, who were perhaps its strongest embodiment, were far from having an idea of a rationalistic economic life.

'The unique creation of ascetic Protestantism alone' was 'an unbroken unity integrating in systematic fashion an ethic of vocation in the world with assurance of religious salvation.'[21] For the Protestant the world was God's creation, endowed with meaning; salvation was certified through work in the world as God's instrument. In the Orient, union with God meant flight from the world. Whilst work became the distinctive form of rational activity in Christian monasticism[22], semi-magical practice remained in Catholicism, which taught that the Church and her sacraments were the means to salvation, thus men were not predestined to salvation or damnation, but could enhance their chances of salvation through ritual. Catholicism also upheld two standards of worldly ethics, of which monastic withdrawal was regarded as the higher.

Samuelsson argues that Weber's examples of the motivations of the Protestant ethic in action, especially Franklin and Baxter, are invalid in terms of the Protestant ethic thesis.[23] His argument misses the point; Weber was not so much concerned with the effects of religious ideas *as such* but with 'those features in the total picture of a religion which has been decisive for the fashioning of the practical way of life'.[24] Inasmuch as Franklin and eighteenth- and nineteenth-century entrepreneurs were motivated by the secular spirit of rational capitalism they were in part demonstrating the *cultural* effects of the Protestant ethic.

The culturology of Protestantism

> The religious root of modern economic humanity is dead . . . Ascetic religiosity has been displaced by a pessimistic though by no means ascetic view of the world, such as that portrayed in Mandeville's *Fable of the Bees* . . . With the complete disappearance of all the remains of the original enormous religious pathos of the sects, the optimism of the Enlightenment . . . appeared as the heir of Protestant asceticism in the field of economic ideas . . . Economic ethics arose against the background of the ascetic ideal; now it has been stripped of its religious import . . . This point had been reached . . . in the 19th century.

Weber thus ends his *General Economic History* with the suggestion that capitalism now has a life of its own which generates its own motivations, it no longer has, nor does it need any religious stimulation to keep it alive.[25]

Protestantism itself contributed to the rationalization and secularization of culture. The ascetic sect broke with patriarchal and authoritarian rule and stressed the isolation of the individual before God. This, according to Weber, formed 'one of the most important foundations of modern "individualism" '.[26]

The culturology of religion is developed in chapter VI of *Economy and Society* in the sections under 'Religious Ethics and the World', discussing economics, politics, sexuality and art.

In discussing Protestant attitudes to the state for example, Weber notes that any ascetic Protestant response to the state and the use of violence involves compromise and ambiguity. The power structure can be an instrument for the rational control of the world, but public political activity involves more of an ethical compromise and relativization of goals than private business enterprise. Weber observes, none the less, that amongst the possible responses to the state is that which is 'One source of the affinity between inner-worldly asceticism and the advocacy of the minimisation of state control such as was represented by the laissez-faire structure of the "Manchester School".'[27]

The puritan sect placed 'individual motive and personal self-interests' in 'the service of maintaining and propagating the "bourgeois" Puritan ethic . . .'[28] 'Only the methodical way of life of the ascetic sects could legitimate and put a halo around the economic "individualist" impulse of the modern capitalist ethic,'[29] Utilitarianism might be seen as the natural successor to the Protestant ethic as the ethical basis of the spirit of capitalism. Nevertheless it would not be fanciful to suggest that a nineteenth-century entrepreneur would still have found an easier 'fit' between utilitarian doctrines and Protestant sectarianism than between utilitarianism and Anglicanism or 'fiesta-laden' Catholicism.[30]

The cultural influence of Protestantism was not confined to economic thought alone. The influence is seen in attitudes towards the sabbath and holy days, education, science and politics, social policy (Weber suggests that the Calvinistic attitude to charity and almsgiving was embodied in Puritan social policy[31]). The changes consequent upon changed attitudes were all highly congruent with the development of the pre-conditions for rational capitalism. The evidence is available in almost any history book covering any part of the period between the Reformation and the Industrial Revolution in England. A striking example of historians' attitudes to Weber is that in three such volumes (*Puritanism and Revolution*; *Society and Puritanism*; *Reformation and Industrial Revolution*) by Christopher Hill, Weber is only once mentioned in any index, this being a reference to a footnote defending Weber against Laski and others.[32]

The Reformation brought liberty of conscience and freedom from traditional authority and casuistry.[33] In England both economic and spiritual monopoly fell, to be replaced by a free market in commodities and doctrines: 'Religious toleration, consumers' choice in religion, is the natural concomitant of the emerging economic order of free industrial production and internal free trade.'[34] However, 'The Calvinist doctrine that the mass of mankind was sinful, that the elect were a minority, fitted the needs of an oligarchical [1657] society much better than this [Quaker] democratic theology.'[35]

The Restoration church provided a means of social control after the revolution. Charles II may have claimed that the Church of England was 'best suited to monarchy',[36] but this 'socially conservative' means of control was no longer controlled by royal office holders.

In a perhaps remarkably cynical passage Weber suggests that the religion of the Reformation became deeply involved in maintaining the status quo for privileged (German) strata. The intellectuals and the masses must now turn to secular means of salvation, he suggested.[37]

The possibility of religion changing its function as other social and economic changes take place has been mentioned by Nottingham;[38] when

> the dominant classes of an earlier period begin to yield
> ground before the challenge of rising classes representing a
> newly emergent political and economic order, religion may
> be a source of creative innovations. Such innovations may
> be temporarily disintegrating, but in the long run often
> contribute to the integration of a different kind of
> society . . .

This hypothesis is clearly applicable to the English Revolution.

Christianity had developed a bureaucratic church with a monarchical head, a church which came to claim a monopoly of the means of grace. It developed a vested interest in the economic and political status quo of the middle ages, demonstrated in 'the salvaging of ecclesiastical power interests, which have increasingly become objectified into a *raison d'église*, by the employment of the same modern instruments of power employed by secular institutions'.[39] It was from this church *and* the social arrangements in which it had a vested interest that Protestants broke. In so doing they not only advanced new ideas, they created new social groups and institutions which were to be important for the rise of capitalism.

The Protestant sect

We have seen in the foregoing section that Weber cites the ascetic Protestant *sect* as the institution maintaining the Protestant ethic. In *The Protestant Sects and the Spirit of Capitalism* (and the long footnotes) Weber examines in some detail the functions of the Protestant sect. This article was seen by the author as continuous with and supplementary to his *Protestant Ethic*.[40]

The Puritan sects 'are the most specific bearers of the inner-worldly form of asceticism. Moreover they are the most consistent antithesis to the universalistic Catholic Church—a compulsory organization for the administration of grace.'[41] The sectarian had to prove himself, holding his own within the sect; 'it is not the ethical doctrine of a religion, but the form of ethical conduct upon which *premiums* are placed that matters' (Weber's emphasis). (The tension between the two structural principles of 'church' and 'sect' *within* Protestantism is mentioned by Weber (p. 314). But in this article he is especially interested in the effects of the voluntaristic principle on conduct.) Three aspects of the sect's life are relevant to Weber's argument. Firstly, partial or whole lay control whereby 'the minister is merely the paid servant of the congregation';[42] secondly 'holding one's own' and thirdly the breeding of 'selected qualities.'[43] The qualities bred by the sect constantly had to be displayed, and one's fellow members were sole judges of satisfactory performance. Membership of the sect had to be achieved and actively maintained. Sanctions such as loss of membership, excommunication, could be brought to bear on members.[44] Thus it was the demands of group membership, the expectations of other members, as much as theological conviction which induced behaviour consistent with the 'Protestant ethic' (and the spirit of capitalism).

Membership was a guarantee of ethical standards; it was also, therefore, a guarantee of credit-worthiness and financial probity.[45] Weber observed, in discussing the secularization of the American sect:[46]

> Today, the kind of denomination to which one belongs is rather irrelevant. . . . What is decisive is that one be admitted to membership by 'ballot' after an *examination* and an ethical *probation* in the sense of the virtues which are at a premium for the inner-worldly asceticism of protestantism . . .

This is discussed in Weber's amusing account of the baptism of the American, which was anticipated by an observer, 'Because he wants to open a bank in M.' Admission to the Baptist congregation

M.W.A.M.S.—G

was given only after a retrospective scrutiny of the candidate's life. Thus, 'Admission to the congregation is recognised as an absolute guarantee of the moral qualities of a gentleman, especially of those qualities required in business matters.[47] Furthermore, 'The whole typically bourgeois ethic was found from the beginning common to all ascetic sects and conventicles and it is identical with the ethic practised by the sects in America up to the very present . . .'[48] Weber then lists prohibited business behaviour for Methodists, including: haggling, charging excessive interest and borrowing without adequate security.

The relative success of Protestants in business is due to the qualities demanded for sect membership. Furthermore some, for example the Quakers, actively gave financial support to members who might otherwise have discredited the sect by going into debt or bankruptcy, Methodist societies have operated in this way in the twentieth century. The mutual aid aspect of the sect was an important form of insurance for both members and their clients.[49]

After the Restoration membership of dissenting religious groups in England had further economic and social consequences. Christopher Hill[50] notes:

> Members of sects evolved a group loyalty in the dark days of persecution in the late seventeenth century. They were likely to deposit their savings within a family or sectarian group. Capital thus remained in industry, not flowing out into the land or funds. The sects inherited a dislike of conspicuous expenditure: their exclusion from the universities and the great world of politics lessened the temptation for sons to dissipate the wealth of their fathers. As communications improved economies of time could release resources for further investment and nonconformists on religious grounds thought time should not be wasted. Moreover, the Quakers especially had far-flung connections, extending in the case of the Barclays from London to Norwich to the Midlands to Philadelphia. This did not make marketing any more difficult. In times of crisis family and sectarian loyalties might save a firm from the failure of confidence which was the main hazard of a growing business. Here was perhaps one of the main contributions of nonconformity to the Industrial Revolution.

Capital was invested by and amongst nonconformists who were debarred from political office and unwilling to live luxuriously. The existence of a network of believers facilitated market relations. Nonconformists' sons unable to enter Oxford or Cambridge devoted themselves to a more scientific and technological education : [51]

> It was a piece of good fortune for England that after 1660 the non-conformist middle class was excluded from Oxford and Cambridge, where they would have learnt to despise science. The connection between dissent and scientific invention was as close in the 18th century as the relation between Baconianism and the Parliamentary cause in the early 17th century.

Virtual exclusion from the cities also dispersed the nonconformists to areas where new industrial enterprises were to grow; providing opportunities for the investment of nonconformist capital and talent.

Voluntary membership of the sect was a cultural factor of some significance also; it indicated a shift from local community-based organization (typified by the parish) to the voluntary association. The guild had united competitors in the local market, the sect united men joined by community of interest. 'These new select groups were united by community of interests rather than geographical propinquity or corporate worship.'[52] As such they prefigured major social institutions in the modern capitalist world.[53]

Conclusion

Weber himself stated that 'The religious root of modern economic humanity is dead; today the concept of the calling is a *caput mortuum* in the world.'[54] His *Protestant Sects and the Spirit of Capitalism* illustrates this point in a discussion of the secularization of the capitalist spirit and of the sect.

The Protestant ethic survived and was expressed in the spirit of capitalism by many nineteenth-century nonconformist English entrepreneurs. The spirit of capitalism, wholly secular, is today distinguished by the sense of economic enterprise as a vocation; work, independence and success are still endowed with moral qualities. The work ethic is shared by many members of disprivileged strata who are thereby, to a degree, integrated into a common enterprise with the entrepreneur (or his successor). The spirit of capitalism is culturally central; it was once peripheral.

In the Carlton Club and at Durham Rotary businessmen meet; participation at the lunch or dinner table depends on proof of ethical conduct. Such associations still serve, 'to diffuse and to maintain the bourgeois capitalist business ethics among a broad strata of the middle classes.'[55]

It is when we examine the so-called underdeveloped nations that we see the full implications of Weber's thesis for Western Europe, and its power to illuminate important areas of social structure. In the underdeveloped countries a majority of the population lives a life 'circumscribed by an immemorial round of traditional agricultural tasks.'[56] The agricultural life is also circumscribed by traditional authority relations and the extended family. The social groups to which men belong are traditional and unquestioned; elders and kin may enforce restraints on any non-traditional activity. Traditional limits may be placed on production and the villager sees no need to produce more than custom demands. The women in the market at Lagos or Freetown are like Weber's 'oriental traders.' This form of trading may constitute a distributive system and provide incomes for women, but it is petty trade and its continuance at any instant is subject to the vicissitudes of family demands.

For the nation to industrialize the villager has to break with tradition and subject himself to the relative insecurity of the impersonal urban market. His success may in part depend on the extent to which he is able to shake off traditional obligations. The workman, as he now is, needs to be motivated to continuous work for a wage, a measure of *dedication* is required.

The dedication may be found in the political party, the nationalist movement or a guerilla army. All these are non-traditional organizations, based on voluntary membership in contrast to the family, clan or village community. Alternatives can be found in urban clan-societies and dedication can be bred through economic inducements, but the problem of breaking with tradition is the same.

Traditional social ties have to be broken, and with them traditional economic motivations and restraints. New orientations to productive work and the market must be induced. The man making this break needs institutional support and will find it in new, voluntaristic associations.

The spirit of capitalism may no longer need a religious basis, but the main features of the spirit of capitalism and rationalistic enterprise are the same as those produced by the Protestant ethic, and the Protestant sect in the seventeenth century.[57]

Notes
1 E. Fischoff, 'The Protestant Ethic and the Spirit of Capitalism: the history of a controversy', in S. N. Eisenstadt, *The Protestant Ethic and Modernisation*, Basic Books, 1968, p. 71.
2 *Ibid.*, p. 72.
3 Weber, *The Protestant Ethic and the Spirit of Capitalism*, Unwin University Books, 1965, p. 91.
4 Weber, *Economy and Society*, ed. G. Roth, Bedminster Press, 1968, vol. II, chapter 16.
5 Weber, *The Protestant Ethic*, p. 47.
6 *Ibid.*
7 *Ibid.*. p. 48.
8 *Ibid.*, p. 97.
9 R. Bendix, *Max Weber: An Intellectual Portrait*, Methuen, 1966.
10 Fischoff, op. cit., p. 81.
11 Weber, *General Economic History*, Part IV and *Economy and Society*, vol. I, pp. 161 ff.
12 B. Nelson, 'Max Weber's sociology of religion', *American Sociological Review*, 1965, p. 596.
13 N. M. Hansen, 'On the sources of economic rationality', in *Zeitschrift für Nationaloeconomie*, no. 4, 1964, pp. 445–55 and 'Early Flemish capitalism', in *Social Research*, 1967, no. 2, pp. 226–48.
14 Weber, *Economy and Society*, p. 480.
15 *Ibid.*, p. 556.
16 H. Trevor-Roper, *Historical Studies*, no. 4, 1965, pp. 18–45.
17 Weber, *Economy and Society*, p. 478.
18 K. Samuelsson, *Religion and Economic Action*, Heinemann, 1961.
19 Hansen, op. cit., p. 447.
20 Weber, *General Economic History*, p. 261.
21 Weber, *Economy and Society*, p. 556.
22 *Ibid.*, pp. 552–6.
23 Weber, *The Protestant Ethic*, chapter 2.
24 'The Protestant sects and the spirit of capitalism', in Gerth and Mills, *From Max Weber*, Routledge & Kegan Paul, 1961, p. 294.
25 *General Economic History*, p. 270.
26 Gerth and Mills, op. cit., p. 321.
27 Weber, *Economy and Society*, p. 583.
28 Gerth and Mills, op. cit., p. 321.
29 *Ibid.*, p. 322.
30 B. Nelson, 'Max Weber's sociology of religion', and 'Conscience and the making of early modern cultures: the Protestant ethic beyond Max Weber', *Social Research*, vol. 36, 1969, pp. 4–21.

31 Weber, *Economy and Society*, p. 589.
32 C. Hill, *Puritanism and Revolution*, Panther, 1968, p. 226.
33 B. Nelson, 'Early modern cultures', *Social Research*, 1969, no. 1, pp. 4–21.
34 C. Hill, *Society and Puritanism*, Panther, 1969, p. 473.
35 *Reformation to Industrial Revolution*, Pelican, 1969, p. 200.
36 *Ibid.*, p. 193.
37 Weber, *Economy and Society*, p. 516.
38 E. K. Nottingham, *Religion and Society*, Random House, 1956, p. 22.
39 Weber, *Economy and Society*, p. 601.
40 Gerth and Mills, op. cit., p. 450 n.1.
41 *Ibid.*, pp. 320–1.
42 C. Hill, *Society and Puritanism*, p. 479.
43 Gerth and Mills, op. cit., pp. 320–1.
44 *Ibid.*, pp. 452–4 nn.8 and 9.
45 *Ibid.*, p. 305.
46 *Ibid.*, p. 307.
47 *Ibid.*, p. 305.
48 *Ibid.*, p. 315.
49 *Ibid.*, p. 308.
50 C. Hill, *Reformation to Industrial Revolution*, p. 246.
51 *Ibid.*, p. 251.
52 *Society and Puritanism*, p. 473.
53 Also especially relevant, *Economy and Society*, chapter 15, section 14.
54 Weber, *General Economic History*, p. 270.
55 Gerth and Mills, op. cit., p. 308.
56 C. Hill, *Reformation to Industrial Revolution*, p. 110.
57 S. N. Eisenstadt (ed.), *The Protestant Ethic and Modernisation*.

Six

J. E. T. Eldridge   **Weber's approach to the
                        sociological study of
                        industrial workers**

Once one has properly if ritualistically acknowledged *The Pro-testant Ethic and the Spirit of Capitalism*,[1] the legacy of Max Weber for the industrial sociologist is usually taken to be his ideal-typical delineations of authority and bureaucracy.[2] The value of the legacy is considerable, although, as Albrow has recently shown, not always well understood even by sympathetic critics.[3] However, the some-what arbitrary way in which Weber's writings have percolated into the English-speaking world has obscured the fact that there is more which may be profitably drawn upon. Georges Friedmann in his book *Industrial Society*[4] provides us with a clue to this when he refers to Weber's 'penetrating essay, little known by specialists', on the psychophysics of industrial labour.[5] Friedmann also notes but does not comment upon another essay in the same volume, namely Weber's 'Methodological Introduction for the survey of the Association for Social Policy, concerning selection and adap-tation (choice and course of occupation) for the workers in large-scale industrial enterprises (1908)'[6] Subsequently both of the essays have been discussed by Anthony Oberschall in his study *Empirical Social Research in Germany, 1848–1914*.[7] Oberschall was concerned to underline just how involved Weber was in trying to understand contemporary social problems in Germany as well as in compara-tive and historical studies. This was reflected in his membership of the Association for Social Policy : a grouping of university teachers, businessmen and civil servants which was concerned to understand the problems created in an industrial society and to recommend reforms in social policy and changes in the law where this was thought desirable and, indeed, to act as a pressure group to that end. The association had been founded in 1872 by the social econo-mists Gustav Schmoller and Adolf Wagner. Weber joined in the 1890s and was at that time much involved with the Association's study of the changing character of labour relations in rural areas in

Germany.[8] The interest of the association in the industrial labour force can be seen, in some ways, as a natural sequel. It was Alfred Weber who first proposed that a survey of industrial workers be undertaken but it was Max who attempted to co-ordinate the research and provide guidance to the social scientists participating in field work. Of the project itself undertaken in the period 1909–11 Oberschall writes:[9]

> In many ways the survey was the most carefully thought through piece of empirical research of the pre-war period (in Germany). Weber spent an entire summer of observation and computation at the textile mill of a relative in preparation for it. His intention was to explore how far the conceptual apparatus and exact measurement techniques developed in the psychological sciences could be fruitfully applied to a study of industrial work on a mass scale and in a natural factory setting . . . The intent was to combine . . . questionnaire data with a systematic exploitation of factory records and direct observation of workers on the factory floor.

For all that Oberschall is constrained to add that as a research undertaking it was too ambitious for the resources available and that, in particular, most workers refused to fill in the questionnaires which were distributed to them. Shades of Marx's *Enquête Ouvrière*![10] If, however, one looks at Weber's 'Methodological Introduction to the Survey', one quickly finds that one is involved in something more than an act of piety. I should now like to dwell upon what I believe to be the nature and significance of that paper.[11] The paper itself is a long one of some 20,000 words and is divided into three sections: (1) an indication of the general character of the survey; (2) the scientific problems of the survey; and (3) the methodology of the survey.

In the first section he indicates that there are two practically intertwined but theoretically separate issues to be pursued:[12]

> The present survey is trying to establish, on the one hand, what effect large-scale industry has on the individual personality, the career and the extra-occupational style of living of the workers, what physical and mental qualities it develops in them, and how these are expressed in the total

behaviour of the workers; and, on the other hand, to what extent industry on its side, in its capacity for development and in the direction of its development is governed by given qualities arising out of the ethnic, social and cultural background, the tradition and the circumstances of the workers.

He then goes on to distinguish between surveys which are socio-political in intent and those which are purely sociological. Most of us are familiar with Weber's views on ethical neutrality through his essay on 'The Meaning of Ethical Neutrality in Sociology and Economics',[13] and here we see them being applied to a concrete research situation. It involves the separation of moral judgment and the advocacy of social policies from attempts to explain problems through causal analysis:[14]

The issue is *not* how social conditions in industry are to be 'assessed' or, in particular, whether the situation in which large-scale industry places workers today is satisfactory or not, whether anyone, and if so, who should take the 'blame' for any unsatisfactory aspects, or what could or should be done to improve it and in what way. No; it is exclusively a matter of the unbiased, objective statement of facts and the ascertainment of their causes in industrial conditions and the individual character of its workers . . . The whole problem at issue—it does not seem superfluous to stress this to my colleagues too—is, socio-politically speaking, a totally *neutral* one by its very nature. From this it follows, for example, that when a researcher, working on one aspect, meets complaints from the workers about any conditions (system of remuneration, conduct of foremen, etc.) in factories, this circumstance would *not*—within the terms of the present survey—concern him as the symptom of a practical 'issue' on which he would have to pronounce judgment: rather it would be taken into consideration simply as the phenomenon attendant upon certain (technical, economic or psychological) transformations whose progress it is his business objectively to *explain*. Considered in this sense, such evidence of the state of mind of the workers could be of significant interest to the present survey. However, the researcher would then have to view them not with regard to their 'justification' but purely with regard to their occurrence. And naturally for expressions of irritation concerning the workers on the part of the employers the same principle applies: they are to be ascertained as *symptoms* of friction in development and analysed when necessary.

The context in which Weber is making these remarks should perhaps be recalled. Weber was during this period engaged in vigorous disputation on matters of social policy with other members of the association under whose auspices the survey was commissioned: in particular with the so-styled academic socialists who advocated the extension of state intervention in and bureaucratic control of economic life. The details do not here concern us[15] but certainly he would not want the report to be used as a vehicle for political opinions which he did not share. He had in 1905, as Simey records,[16] spoken to the Association on the very subject of industrial relations in large-scale undertakings where he had argued that workers who went on strike without having given the notice required by law should not therefore be pilloried as 'immoral' or 'irresponsible'. It was the law itself which was at fault because German labour law with its accompanying punishments and reprimands implied the subordination of one party to another and as such tended to deprive working men of their liberty. And in the 'Methodological Introduction' he explicitly says that one should not *assume* that the problems of industrial relations are susceptible to legislative solutions, as if to counteract existing conventional beliefs on the subject. At the same time he clearly did not believe that this approach of the 'pure sociologist' was divorced from practical affairs. He saw such work as a means of spreading enlightenment to replace unsubstantiated beliefs and, in this respect, existing assumptions on the part of various interested parties might be examined and possibly in the light of causal analysis modified by those who hold them. Not that this would necessarily lead to compromise or consensus between the various interest groups but rather that some kind of sociological boundaries concerning what was or was not possible might be drawn. It is a reflection of his position expressed in 'Ethical Neutrality'[17] that:

The sciences, both normative and empirical, are capable of

rendering an inestimable service to persons engaged in political activity by telling them that (1) these and these 'ultimate' positions are conceivable with reference to a practical problem; (2) such and such are the facts which you must take into account in making your choice between these positions.

It is, however, worth noting that at the very end of the 'Methodological Introduction' he does make explicit that he shared the view of Alfred Weber, namely that the impact of large-scale industry on the life of workmen, both within the work place and in their life style, was independent of whether such industry was capitalist or socialist in organization. Weber's view on the matter has a good deal in common with Engels as expressed in the latter's essay on authority:[18]

> The automatic machinery of a big factory is much more despotic than the small capitalists who employ workers ever have been. At least with regard to hours of work one may write upon the portals of these factories: *Lasciate ogni autonomia, voich'eutrate* (Leave, ye that enter in, all autonomy behind). If man, by dint of his knowledge and inventive genius, has subdued the force of nature, the latter avenge themselves upon him by subjecting him, in so far as he employs them, to a veritable despotism, independent of all social organization. Wanting to abolish authority in large-scale industry is tantamount to wanting to abolish industry itself, to destroy the power loom in order to return to the spinning wheel.

Manifestly for Engels this did not render redundant arguments concerning the relative merits of capitalist and socialist industrial societies. Likewise in Weber's case, by drawing attention to certain similarities in societies with machine technologies, he is not to be interpreted as propounding a convergence theory concerning industrial societies. On the contrary, true to his voluntaristic position he states:[19]

> the substitution of *any* form of common economic solidarity for today's selection on the principle of private economic *viability*, chaining as it does the whole existence of those confined within the factory, whether directing or

> obeying, to the outcome of the employers' *private* cost and
> profit calculations, would radically change the spirit found
> today in this great edifice, and no-one can even surmise
> with what consequences.

The remainder of the first section goes on to consider the necessity of understanding certain economic, technical and organiza-
tional facts as a prerequisite of a successful sociological study.
For example, the actual pattern of sales distribution may affect
the degree to which a product may be standardized and this will
have implications for the qualities required in a labour force.
Again, if one can indicate the firms and industries in which wage
costs constitute a high proportion of total capital costs, or where
current methods of production involve such things as high wastage
of materials, excessive machine wear or a high percentage of flaws
and irregularities in the final product, one may postulate that the
incentive to implement technical changes is considerable. The
question then to be considered in relation to the labour force is
what effect this has on the number of workers required and
whether the need is for better qualified or less well qualified
workers in consequence of technical change. One does not assume
therefore that technical change necessarily implies a debasement
of skill.

One should not be surprised to find this painstaking concern for
non-sociological facts in Weber's discussion (and including, as we
note below, a concern with physiological and psychological data).
It is consistent with his view expressed in *Theory of Social and
Economic Organization*[20] that

> statistics of phenomena devoid of meaning such as death
> rates, phenomena of fatigue, the production rate of
> machines . . . because they are not 'understandable' are
> naturally not on that account any less important. This is
> true even for sociology in the present sense which restricts
> itself to subjectively understandable phenomena . . . They
> become conditions, stimuli furthering or hindering
> circumstances of action.

What Weber does go on to suggest as a matter of research
strategy is that, in so far as the survey is concerned to discover
differences in aptitude as between workers, one might look at

firms where the following three factors co-exist: (1) where wage costs are a high percentage of total costs (since the need to maintain or improve on profits necessitates a careful policy of labour utilization and hence recruitment); (2) production situations where standards of quality and quantity are especially dependent on the aptitudes of workers; and (3) product standardization since this provides the best chance for measuring the output of workers. However, even in an empirical situation which approximated to that just outlined, one could not simply treat the structure of the labour force as a dependent variable:[21]

> It should also be asked whether and in what sense the industry concerned for its part finds itself (or imagines itself) restricted in the manner of its realization of capital, e.g. in the trend to increasing capital investment in general, to standardisation, to increasing speed of turnover, etc., by given qualities of its labour force, because these qualities impede technical innovations of a certain type.

This leads Weber to stress the importance of analysing the character of local labour markets on both the demand and supply side together with the actual modes of recruitment which a firm employs. This is linked up with his parallel interest in trying to chart what constitutes typical occupational career patterns:[22]

> To ascertain as accurately as possible from which other *jobs* the individual categories of workers in the factories concerned were recruited, would be of quite special interest, especially in industries where vast expansion or rapid technical transformation is taking place here. From our point of view, the occupational career of the workers would appear as a kind of 'military road' on which, from particular geographical, ethnic, social and cultural starting points (which should be more closely examined) they have advanced to their qualifications for the job they finally attain.

This point is worth emphasizing not least because studies of labour mobility still rarely get anywhere near the sequential approach advocated here. Dubin, for example, in his discussion of individual job mobility points out that 'stable data on a substantial number of working life histories simply do not exist'.[23] Similarly, Robinson has recently written of the 'desperate dearth of adequate information about the working of local labour markets'.[24] And what is needed? 'Not only improved . . . economic and statistical information but also . . . more knowledge about the sociological and psychological factors affecting people's choice of jobs and their job changes.'[25] This comment came, one may observe, almost exactly sixty years after Weber's paper. One should recognize also that even if there proved to be differences in aptitude that could be traced back to such factors as age, sex, geographical, ethnic or social background, the character of the training given by individual firms could act as a significant intervening variable. This aspect by itself might demand very detailed empirical study. This Weber clearly recognized but at the same time he saw various micro-studies as feeding into an overall appraisal of the impact of large-scale industry on society. The essential sociological questions to be considered in this respect were:[26]

(1) How far the evolution of the working class is moving in the direction of qualitative, and, influenced by this economic and social distinctions of its various classes, or conversely, in the direction of increasing uniformity: (2) how far the utility of the individual industrial worker appears increasingly *specialized*, tailored to the exclusive use of quite special individual qualities, or conversely, *universalistic*: (3) to what extent individual industries are correspondingly increasingly *emancipating* themselves from certain qualities of their workers, be they due to practice and training, and how far any 'standardization' of products means a 'standardization' of the workers as well, or conversely how far specialized equipment means a multiplicity of qualities in the workers; (4) furthermore, what are the chances of promotion for the workers within particular types of occupation both economically (according to the possible shape of their earnings curve) and organizationally (according to the degree of relative responsibility or even *superiority* which may in the course of their careers succeed the at first inevitable subordination) and psychologically (according to their subjective inclination with regard to the individual posts they have the opportunity to hold) . . . lastly (5) how the result of all these influences

affects the psycho-physical and typical characteristics of the workers of an industry, and their style of living.

Throughout this passage we see that Weber is keeping the options open as to what precisely was happening to the industrial working class but at all events he is taking into account both objective structural factors—the composition of capital, the operation of labour markets for example—and subjective definitions of the situation which might, say, colour employers' attitudes to technical change or the aspirations and ambitions of employees.

In the second section on the scientific problems of the survey, Weber essentially is concerned to work through the difficulties of demonstrating what may count as a viable explanation of the level of a worker's effort and output. The nearest equivalent to a discussion of this sort in English is incidentally to be found in W. Baldamus, *Efficiency and Effort*.[27] While obviously sympathetic to the work going on in physiology and experimental psychology on the nature of rhythm acquisition differences in the individual's psychophysical equipment, the nature of fatigue, and so on, Weber was very doubtful about how fruitfully such work could be applied to solve his problems. Since, however, different kinds of work could be expected to make different kinds of demands upon the central nervous system he contemplated the possibility of surveying general practitioners with a view to finding out the incidence of neuroses with reference to occupational and industrial background. And he also accepted that it would be of great importance if one could show that there was a physiological basis for indicating the effects of job changing on output. There might prove to be economic advantages which outweigh those which are commonly held to accrue to extensive job specialization.

But essentially Weber's position is that physiological factors could never of themselves provide a sufficient explanation of worker behaviour. Decisive motivation will be located elsewhere when one looks at why workers behave as they do. At times considerations of economic rationality appear to dominate as in the case of the young man who changes his job to further his skills and enhance the market value of his labour. Yet this is by no means always the case. It was a matter of common observation that men both remained in jobs when financially better ones were available and changed jobs even when there was no economic gain from so doing. In other words worker motivation was a complex social phenomenon not reducible to physiological laws.

What we have already said indicates that for Weber there was a level of sociological explanation sui generis and that reductionist explanations (notwithstanding his own methodological individualism) were to be eschewed. He develops his position with particular force when he comes to consider the status of biological inheritance as an explanation of a worker's ability in his job. He referred scathingly to the 'chaos of unverifiable assertions' that existed concerning the role of inheritance as an explanation of individual or indeed racial differences noting that many so-called biological explanations were more appropriately attributable to tradition and adding, 'the totally woolly conventional concept of the "folk character", as the "source" of particular qualities of the working class, inextricably unites these too vastly differing things.' Further, when one notes how far a particular industrial community adheres to tradition and how far it adapts to innovation, there are certain structural questions which may be asked. One must not only examine whether changes in the social and economic structure of a society and changes in modes of production are resisted by traditionalists in communities where such transformations take place, but whether indeed population changes and migratory movements make it possible to use terms like 'adherence to tradition' or 'adaptation to innovations' in a realistic way, let alone ascribe these responses to 'inherited characteristics'.

Weber develops the point that before resorting to biological explanations of observed differences in individual or group behaviour one should as a matter of research strategy exhaust other alternatives at a social and cultural level. Indeed one could not have any real confidence in biological explanations unless this were done. The importance of environmental factors is indicated particularly during the formative period of youth.[28]

> Such influences . . . as exerted among other things by type of nourishment and upbringing, degree of incentive and opportunity, for intellectual activity and the richness of experience offered by the milieu of the youthful years. The wealth and poverty of material circumstances and the 'spiritual horizon' of the home, determined chiefly by the social class of the parents, school education and military

service, the population and economic and cultural character of the home town, or town where youth was spent, and their early experiences at work, exert, in all probability, such a tenacious influence on the direction followed by development, and on the development or suppression of individual capabilities that only *very* considerably above-average gifts for particular activities seem to have the ability to make themselves felt to any recognizable extent in the face of the conditions, determined by the social and cultural class structure, which held sway during the period of maximum plasticity.

Comment such as this would appear to have renewed relevance at the present time when there appears to be something of a growing fashion to explain social behaviour in biological terms.

The significance of social factors in explaining worker behaviour is underlined in the final section on the methodology of the survey. This comes out with particular clarity in Weber's discussion of the relations between methods of wage payment and worker output. The nature of this linkage he holds to be of great importance: [29]

In an extraordinarily large number of cases where it was thought our own dealing with unchangeable qualities in a particular labour force, be they inbred or determined by tradition and environment in particular with mentally or physically determined limits to their working *capability* which were laid down once and for all, changes in the remuneration system have shown, after sufficient time has elapsed for their efforts to become apparent, that in effect the manner of their interest in the quantity or quality of their work was the decisive factor. In addition there were far-reaching consequences which the differences in remuneration systems entail for the degree of incentive for the individual classes of workers in a factory, in their relationships to one another, to works managers, foremen, comrades engaged in the same piece-work etc. The whole internal structure of the working process and the formation of social groups . . . are intimately connected with the system of remuneration.

By stressing how important it was for researchers to look at systems of wage payment he had in mind the possibility of collecting data which might permit one to consider questions such as the following:

(1) How far are wage systems consciously designed to achieve certain kinds of results—in terms of the quality and quantity of work. In this sense one might compare the extent of such rational as compared to traditional forms of payment in Germany industry.

This is a relatively simple application of Weber's well-known distinction between social action which was a product of habituation and that based upon a technical means-and-end calculation.

(2) How far do rational systems of wage payment actually achieve their ends? Here we have an illustration of the distinction between subjective and objective rationality discussed by Weber in 'Ethical Neutrality':[30]

> A *subjectively* rational action is not identical with a rationally 'correct' action . . . Rather, it means only that the subjective intention of the individual is planfully directed to the means which are regarded as correct for a given end . . . An increase in subjectively rational conduct can lead to objectively more 'efficient' conduct but it is not inevitable.

There might, for example, be unanticipated consequences which could lead to restriction of output. Or again one might compare the extent to which workers grouped according to religious, ethnic, or other specified social factors together with geographical background responded differently to a similar system of remuneration.[31]

(3) What effects on the stability and level of output may be observed following specified changes in a system of remuneration?

(4) If one held the system of remuneration constant what earnings curve could be observed for individual workers over an extended period of time? This could provide a basis for comparisons between occupations. It might also permit intra-occupational comparisons in which the attempt might be made to assess how far significant differences between individuals were associated with specific differences in ethnic, social or cultural backgrounds.

Each of these questions, however, depended on researchers obtaining not only the relevant statistics but statistics which they could meaningfully interpret. Weber's advice on this is very down to earth and without doubt still relevant to researchers in this area:[32]

> Colleagues cannot be urgently enough enjoined to sit down at the wage books *themselves*, wherever possible, and to carry out at least some of the admittedly to a large extent purely mechanical work of making extracts *themselves*. In my personal experience a few dozen pads of pay chits or effective power tables carefully gone through and worked out by the researcher himself and discussed in every detail with the director or his representative, afford him a far more certain judgment of co-efficients of output, especially of the questions of to what extent power over the very different and often complicated incentives contained in the form of remuneration is influenced by materials, machines, changes in type of occupation, interruption of work, braking on the part of the worker, or in times of stagnation, on the part of the factory (by means of the practice, so common nowadays in this event of fixing a maximum output quota) finally, of the degree and direction in which, after all these circumstances have been taken into account, the individual personalities of the workers actually determines the path of his earnings curve, than the most comprehensive set of statistics, fine tho' they might be, compiled for him by someone *else*.

All of this is in line with the view expressed in the psycho-physics of industrial labour that if one wanted to understand the factors effecting labour productivity it was more fruitful to undertake case study work in which one analysed individual production and earnings curves rather than working with group totals and averages. This is very much in line with the view recently expressed by the labour economist Derek Robinson in his attempt to give a more realistic appraisal of the working of labour markets, in the paper cited above.[33] Robinson argues that macro-analysis of wage studies is an unsuitable approach to earnings analysis precisely because such aggregate studies do not uncover the divergencies of change which exist at the plant or micro-level. Even studies of average earnings within a firm which do not take account of changes in skill mix or occupational groupings are, he suggests, of dubious usefulness.

Towards the end of the 'Methodological Introduction' Weber raises a whole cluster of questions about the relationship between occupational career (or fate) and life style. Essentially they are the kinds of questions which sociologists in this country have been asking recently in examining the embourgeoisement thesis.[34] For example, the better paid workers in Germany, Weber noted, might be similar in incomes and even educational background to junior civil servants, clerks and members of the petty bourgeoisie. But did they manifest similar modes of family life, patterns of leisure, religious affiliations? Further, within the working class as a whole could differences in 'life style' be observed and if so what criteria existed to account for them?[35]

In the lands of the Anglo-Saxon there is often not the slightest social contact between skilled trade unionists and lower classes of worker—it is well known that they sometimes find it hard to sit at the same table. It would be of considerable interest to investigate how far, and why, these differentiations exist in Germany, or are coming into being, or conversely are in the process of disappearing; likewise, naturally, for marriages and general social relations with junior office workers and petty bourgeoisie.

I think we may safely conclude that 1908 was a good year for industrial sociology, at least in terms of what was on the agenda.

Notes:

1   Weber, *The Protestant Ethic and the Spirit of Capitalism*, Allen & Unwin, 1947.
2   See particularly Weber, *Theory of Social and Economic Organization*, 1947.
3   See M. Albrow, *Bureaucracy*, Macmillan, 1970, especially chapters 2 and 3.
4   G. Friedmann, *Industrial Society*, Free Press, 1955.
5   Weber, 'Zur Psychophysik der Industriellen Arbeit', in *Gesammelte Aufsätze zur Soziologie und Sozialpolitik*, J. C. B. Mohr, Tübingen, 1924.
6   Weber, 'Methodologische Einleitung für die Ehrebungen der Vereins für Sozialpolitik über Auslese und Anpassung (Berufewahlen und Berufsschicksal) der Arbeiteschaft des geschlossenen Grossindustrie', in *Gesammelte Aufsätze zur Soziologie und Sozialpolitik*.
7   A. Oberschall, *Empirical Social Research in Germany, 1848–1914*, Mouton-Paris, 1965. See particularly chapter 6, 'Max Weber and the problem of industrial work'.

8 See Weber's 'Die Verhältrnisse der Landarbeiter im obstelbischen Deutschland' in *Schriften der Vereins für Sozialpolitik*, vol. LV, Duncker & Humblot, Berlin, 1892. There is a brief exposition of this in R. Bendix, *Max Weber: An Intellectual Portrait*, Methuen, 1966, chapter 2.

9 Op. cit., p. 8.

10 See T. B. Bottomore and M. Rubel, *Karl Marx. Selected Writings in Sociology and Philosophy*, Pelican, 1963, pp. 210–18.

11 The English translation of this paper has been made by D. M. Hytch. This is now available in J. E. T. Eldridge (ed.), *Max Weber: the Interpretation of Social Reality*, Michael Joseph, 1971.

12 *Ibid.*, p. 104.

13 In Weber's *The Methodology of the Social Sciences*, Free Press, 1949.

14 J. E. T. Eldridge (ed.), op. cit., pp. 104–5.

15 For a useful recent account see T. S. Simey, *Social Science and Social Purpose*, Constable, 1968, chapter 5.

16 Op. cit., pp. 97–8.

17 'Ethical neutrality', p. 10.

18 F. Engels, 'On authority', in L. S. Feuer (ed.), *Marx and Engels: Basic Writings on Politics and Philosophy*, Fontana, 1969, pp. 520–1.

19 J. E. T. Eldridge (ed.), op. cit., p. 155.

20 Weber, *Theory of Social and Economic Organization*, Free Press, 1964, p. 100.

21 J. E. T. Eldridge (ed.), op. cit., p. 110.

22 *Ibid.*, p. 111.

23 R. Dubin, *The World of Work*, Prentice-Hall, 1958, p. 266.

24 D. Robinson, 'Wage drift, fringe benefits and manpower distribution', *OECD*, 1968, p. 167.

25 *Ibid.*, p. 167.

26 J. E. T. Eldridge (ed.), op. cit., p. 115.

27 W. Baldamus, *Efficiency and Effort*, Tavistock, 1961.

28 J. E. T. Eldridge (ed.), op. cit., p. 129.

29 *Ibid.*, p. 137.

30 W. Baldamus, *Efficiency and Effort*, pp. 34–5.

31 For an example of just such an approach see M. Dalton, 'The industrial "rate buster": a characterisation', *Applied Anthropology*, vol. 7, no. 1, 1948; and O. Collins, M. Dalton and D. Roy, 'Restriction of output and social cleavage in industry', *Applied Anthropology*, vol. 5, no. 3, 1946.

32 J. E. T. Eldridge (ed.), op. cit., p. 142.

33 D. Robinson, 'Wage drift, fringe benefits and manpower distribution'.

34 See particularly, J. H. Goldthorpe, D. Lockwood, F. Bechoffer and J. Platt, *The Affluent Worker*, vols 1–3, Cambridge University Press, 1968–9; I. C. Cannon, 'Ideology and occupational community', *Sociology*, vol. 1, no. 2, May 1967; and W. G. Runciman, *Relative Deprivation and Social Justice*, Routledge & Kegan Paul, 1966.

35. J. E. T. Eldridge (ed.), op. cit., p. 151.